Paris With Kids

ISBN: 1-4392-6899-1
ISBN-13: 9781439268995

Paris With Kids

Alison Ryan

2010

Dedication

This book is dedicated to my sister Tracey, my best friend for life and the person who encouraged me to write this book.

Table of Contents

Chapter 1
Bonjour, Paris!

"I've got news," said my husband John one evening in January of 2001, as we stood side-by-side at the sink washing the dinner dishes.

"What kind of news?" I asked.

"News about my next assignment," he said flatly.

I immediately dried my hands on the dishtowel and turned towards him. "Why didn't you bring this up at the dinner table?"

"I hesitate to bring it up at all," he said, reaching for another dish and submerging it in the soapy water.

"Why is that?" I asked.

"Because you know how you get, Alison," he said with a frown.

I had married a military man, which meant that somebody we didn't even *know* in San Antonio, Texas, got to decide where and when we'd move next. And even though my husband made a yearly list of his top three choice destinations, rarely did we ever end up where we thought we would. I figured from his tone of voice that it was bad news.

"Well, out with it," I said.

He hesitated a bit, clearly choosing his words carefully. "I don't want you to get too excited," he said finally. "It's still not one hundred percent certain…." His voice trailed off.

In an instant, my feelings of dread disappeared. A rush of adrenalin hit me, causing my heart to pound hard in my chest. "Wait a minute," I said, "what are you talking about?"

He finally turned to face me and said the words I never thought I'd hear come out of his mouth: "The Paris job."

My head was spinning. My husband and I had discussed "the Paris job" six months ago. It was a position in a small NATO office on the outskirts of Paris. The assignment was for two years, and the government would take care of moving all our possessions, including our car, overseas for us. At the time John told me it was "very unlikely" he'd get the job. However, the mere fact that he was bringing it up again meant that it was now *fairly likely* he would get the job.

Full color, 3-D images of the City of Lights flooded my brain. I pictured myself dressed in chic French clothing and carrying a baguette in my hand, walking serenely through the Tuileries garden while Parisian street musicians played in the background.

"Hey, hey, hello?" John said, waving his hand in front of my face. "Earth to Alison."

I was immediately wrenched out of my Parisian daydream and back into reality. "Mmmm—-?" I mumbled.

"I told you not to get too excited," my husband said sternly. "It's still not one hundred percent certain. So don't go making any plans."

"Oh, of course not," I said, dreamily.

"In fact," he continued, "I wouldn't even mention it to anyone, not even your sister."

"Sure," I readily agreed.

I was euphoric. A euphoria that lasted for several months and was only enhanced when, in early June, we flew to Paris for a two-week vacation. It was supposed to be a "working vacation" for my husband. He was there to attend the Paris Air show as a representative from his office (which means it was basically an all-expense-paid vacation with a little business thrown in). And luckily, the business was conducted *à la française* at extravagant dinners and cocktail parties thrown by the huge conglomerates who were interested in selling their wares to anyone who could afford them. I had never seen so much elegant food in one place. Champagne flowed endlessly out of expensive, French labeled bottles toted by an army of tuxedoed waiters. *I could certainly get used to this*, I thought to myself as I surveyed the scene at one particularly lavish affair.

Later on that week while I was out shopping, John visited the office where he would work (should he get the job) for an informal interview with his prospective boss. "How did it go?" I asked when we met back at our hotel that afternoon.

"Very well," he said with a knowing smile. "So well, in fact, that I'd like to take you to dinner to celebrate." We headed out on the metro to a cozy little bistro in the Seventeenth Arrondissement. After dinner, as darkness began to descend on the City of Lights, my husband suggested we forego the metro and walk home.

"All the way to our hotel?" I asked, a bit perplexed. "That's pretty far away."

"Just indulge me for a bit," he said and winked at me.

As we strolled along Avenue Victor Hugo in one of the wealthiest neighborhoods in Paris, I couldn't help but comment on the regal looking apartment buildings that lined the street. "Just look at that sculpted stone balcony," I said.

"And that one," said my husband pointing to a balcony outlined in black, wrought iron scrolls. Some of the buildings actually had glass front doors allowing us to see inside the lobby. One featured a pristine white marble floor covered with lush red carpet that was trimmed with gold tassels.

"That must be quite the life," I mused.

Suddenly, John stopped in the middle of the sidewalk, turned to face me, grabbed both my hands in his, and stared intently into my eyes.

"What if it was *our* life?"

"What are you talking about?" I said.

"This neighborhood is where the majority of the Embassy apartments are located. If I get this job, we'll be given the use of an apartment normally reserved for State Department personnel. An apartment just like one of these," he said, pointing all around him.

I could hardly believe what I was hearing.

"And do you know what the best part would be? I could walk to work. Imagine that." He smiled down at me. "Imagine what kind of amazing commute that would be, walking past the Arc de Triomphe every day!"

"Now, don't get too excited," I admonished him, "this still isn't one hundred percent certain."

He laughed at my attempt to mock him. "You know what?" he said with a mischievous smile. "At this point, I think it's about ninety-nine percent certain."

Two months after we returned from our trip to France, we got some exciting news; but it wasn't exactly the news we were expecting. I found out I was pregnant with our first child. Baby Ryan was due to make his or her debut on or before April 30, 2002.

"It'll be good for her to spend her first few months stateside before the upheaval of the move," commented my husband.

"So, not only are you certain you're getting the job," I teased him, "you're also certain it's a 'her,' huh?"

"I'm one hundred percent certain it's a girl," he said, "and I'm ninety-nine point nine percent certain I'm getting the Paris job." Turns out he was right on both counts. Three months later, John's boss told him we were moving to Paris that summer, and six months after that our daughter Carole was born.

The three months before our move was truly a whirlwind. We sold our home, watched all our worldly goods be sealed in huge crates, and embarked on a multistate tour in an effort to visit as many relatives as possible before leaving the country. Then there was the mad rush to secure our newborn daughter a passport in time for our flight to Paris. It was delivered to us a mere twenty-four hours before departure. As our flight lifted off from Dulles Airport en route to our new life in Paris, I gazed down at Carole sleeping contentedly between us.

"Are you ready to begin your French adventure, girlfriend?" I asked the sleeping baby, whose mouth suddenly curled up in an involuntary smile. Clearly, she was.

Chapter 2
Our Paris Apartment

We were given the keys to our Paris apartment on a Friday in late September, and I could hardly contain my excitement. I wanted to go over there immediately and check out our new digs. John, however, insisted that we wait until the next day. So, early Saturday morning we anxiously walked up Boulevard Malesherbes scanning the buildings for number fifty-two. When we finally located it, we stopped in our tracks and just stared at it in awe from across the street.

We knew we were on the fifth floor (which in France actually means the sixth floor since they count the ground floor as floor *zéro*). As the Saturday morning traffic whizzed past us, we stood on the sidewalk, carefully counting the rows of windows on the building opposite us. "That's it, that's the one!" my husband said excitedly. "Can you see it? It's the one with the wrought iron railing along the balcony."

"It has a balcony?" I said, squinting in the sunlight.

"Let's go," he said. I grabbed hold of the stroller with our sleeping four-month-old and we sprinted across the street.

Once in front of number fifty-two, we pushed open an enormous wooden door and entered a long, cavernous hallway lined with tall, white, Grecian columns. It was paved with cobblestones and had a high, vaulted ceiling. On the left was an elegant, glass-paneled door with a large gold A imprinted on it. We pushed it open and stepped into the lobby. The gray marble floor was covered with a lush red floral carpet that reached all the way to the steps. We walked over to the base of the winding staircase and looked up: six flights of stairs stretched out before us.

"Thank God for that elevator," I sighed. It took a bit of maneuvering to get the stroller, my six-and-a-half-foot tall husband, and myself inside the small space. Once we did, John (the only one with a free hand) pushed the button for the fifth floor, and the elevator hummed to life.

It took off with a jerk and travelled noisily and slowly up to the fifth floor. Upon exiting the elevator, we discovered two large, wood-paneled doors, one on each side of the hallway. Neither one had any markings on it: no name, no numbers, no letters, nothing. "Which one is ours?" I asked my husband.

"Well," he said, slowly examining the collection of bizarre-looking keys that had been given to us, "we could simply try the keys in one of the doors. If they fit, then we'll know the apartment is ours." It seemed like a good idea at the time. Of course, neither one of us anticipated that one—or both—of the apartments might be already occupied.

As we stood in the quiet of the hallway trying to insert key after key into the lock, Carole woke up and started to wail. Her crying echoed through the empty hallway and down the cavernous stairwell to the floors below. "Quiet her down," whispered my husband, "it's still early." I took my daughter out of her stroller and started to pace back and forth while gently rocking her in my arms. Suddenly, the door opposite us opened, and I found myself face-to-face with a pale, dark haired woman with a very severe pageboy haircut. "*Que faites vous?*" she sneered at me.

"Uhhhh...," I stuttered, wholly unprepared to be confronted by a native French speaker at such an early hour. Even though I was fluent in the language, try as I might I could not utter a single word.

My husband, sensing that I was frozen by fear and unable to speak, attempted to explain our presence in the hallway. "*Nous sommes vos nouveaux voisins,*" he said with a broad smile. I'm not sure if it was his heavy American accent or his smile that did it, but the woman, whose ghostly skin tone and head-to-toe black attire made her look like Morticia Adams, screwed up her face in disgust and shouted, "*Quoi?*"

In an instant my brain freeze was over and I found myself explaining in my most polite Parisian accented French that we were, in fact, the new occupants of the apartment opposite her own. Apparently my French was more pleasing to her ear than my husband's because her scowl disappeared and the expression on her face became one of bored indifference (an expression I would become very familiar with over the next five years since it's the expression most Parisians wear on a daily basis). She stood there for a full thirty seconds looking us up and down, taking in every detail of our attire before opening her mouth to speak again. Then she did something most Parisians do once they realize they are talking to Americans; she spoke to us in English. "You are American, *non?*"

"Yes!" blurted out my husband, happy to be participating in the conversation again.

"Embassy?" she asked. Again, my husband answered in the affirmative.

"Your apartment is over there," she said pointing a bony finger towards the huge window on the opposite wall that looked out onto the courtyard. We both let out a gasp. Then she pointed her bony finger over my shoulder to the door of the apartment we had been desperately trying to open with our keys. "That apartment is already occupied." And with that, she turned her back on us and slammed the door shut in our faces with a mighty *thwack*.

We stood there in shock, staring at the closed door for a full ten seconds before I turned to my husband and said, "Welcome to Paris."

"You can't really blame her for being upset," he said, as we rode the elevator back down to the lobby. "It is rather early on a Saturday morning."

"Yes," I agreed, "and she thought she had caught someone breaking and entering. Quick, let's get out of here before she calls the *gendarmes*."

"Don't be ridiculous," John admonished me. "We're here to check out our new home. And this time, I think I know how to find the right apartment." He held out a small, white tag that was tied with string to the mass of keys we had been given. "See this?" he said. "It says '*Escalier* C.'" He then pointed to the large gold C imprinted on the front of the door across the courtyard. "*Escalier* C, staircase C. We were in the wrong building."

The lobby we entered into was a mirror image of the one across the courtyard. It had the same lush floral carpet, the same winding staircase, and the same noisy elevator that we rode, once again, up to the fifth floor. Upon exiting, we hesitated in front of two identical doors that, like their counterparts across the courtyard, had no markings on them at all. "Now what?" I asked.

"Well, the tag also says something else I can't translate; take a look."

I took it from his hands. It read, in French, *Fifth floor right.*

"Then it must be this one," said my husband as he inserted the key into the lock of the door on our immediate right. He rotated the key once, and we heard a soft click. Slowly the door swung open.

"Oh my goodness," I said as we entered our new home. The ceilings were at least fifteen feet high, and the gorgeous, honey-colored hardwood floors were laid out in a herringbone pattern. They creaked beneath our feet as we wandered silently through the hallway. It turned left and right in a bizarre zigzag pattern that, in the end, left us wondering where the front door was.

"Great," I said, "we're lost in our own apartment."

"Well, with no furniture and nothing on the walls, there's not much to distinguish one hallway from another," observed my husband.

After arriving at a few dead ends, we finally navigated our way back to the front door. As John prepared to change Carole's diaper on the floor, I wandered a few steps away into the cavernous living room, where sunlight streamed through the floor-to-ceiling windows. Against the far wall stood a large marble fireplace with intricate scrolls carved up and down each side. The ceilings were covered with the most exquisite crown molding I had ever seen. Angels playing harps and flutes and lyres were carved into it, and in each corner was carved a vase holding a bouquet of flowers. It was as if we had entered a time machine that transported us back to eighteenth century Paris.

I giggled as I stood there, trying to imagine how our Jennifer Convertibles couch and La-Z-Boy recliner would look against the backdrop of so much elegance. "So," asked my husband, his voice dripping with sarcasm, "does the apartment meet with *madame's* approval?"

"Well." I rolled my eyes. "If this is the best you can manage, *monsieur*, I guess it will have to do."

And with that we packed up our diaper bag and headed out the door. "Of course, the most exciting part is yet to come," John said as we strolled back down Boulevard Malesherbes.

"And that is?" I asked.

"Watching all our stuff moved in, of course. You saw that size of that elevator. Those poor movers are going to have to haul everything up six flights of stairs!"

Good grief, I thought, *that will be a drama in itself.* Unfortunately, moving in was only the beginning of the drama we would experience living in Paris.

Chapter 3
Adventures in Obstetrics and Gynecology

After eighteen months of living in Paris, I became pregnant with my second child, and after much discussion with friends, I chose an obstetrician. Dr. Mellerio was an older gentleman who had been in practice for more than thirty years. He had four children of his own, pictures of whom he proudly displayed on his desk, and his relaxed demeanor immediately put me at ease.

Our first meeting was, for me at least, simply a testing of the waters. Would I like him? Would I agree with his philosophy on pregnancy and childbirth? And most importantly, would I be able to understand what he was saying? While I considered myself fluent in conversational French, when it came to specialized areas of discussion, I often found myself at a loss for words. My first order of business was to express my concerns about my lack of fluency in this particular area.

"I speak French," I told him, "but not gynecological French."

Dr. Mellerio laughed. "But I speak very good English," he assured me, in *heavily* accented English, and then proceeded to speak to me only in French. In fact, those were the only words he ever said to me in English. He took copious notes as I related my medical history up until that point in my life. Our conversation was of the typical new-patient-information-gathering variety; however, the fact that the physician himself was recording the information was a bit of a surprise.

Then, the situation became even stranger. The phone rang. Dr. Mellerio stopped speaking in mid-sentence and answered it. What followed was an intimate and detailed conversation between doctor and patient that I wished I hadn't been present for. After he hung up, he began questioning me again, as if nothing had happened. *Well, okay,* I thought, *perhaps it was an emergency.* But less than five minutes later, the phone at his desk rang again; again he answered it and began dispensing medical advice to the patient at the other end of the line. Now I was truly intrigued. *How does he get any work done if he's constantly taking phone calls?* I thought. *How are we ever going to finish this appointment if he keeps stopping to take calls?*

This was my first experience with the way French physicians manage their patients. In general, they do not have anyone to "screen" calls for them to find out the nature of a patient's question. They simply have the calls put through to them in their office or, as in the case of my child's pediatrician, give out their cell phone number! Yes, shockingly enough, Carole's pediatrician gave me his cell phone number at our first meeting and told me to call him if I "needed anything." I assumed he meant in the case of a medical emergency and thus tucked the number away somewhere figuring I'd rarely have use for it. But lo and behold at our first appointment, his cell phone rang constantly and he, too, took every single call, placing my child and me in a state of limbo as he conversed with parent after parent about everything from stuffy noses to broken bones. Clearly years of multitasking in this manner had made him an expert at it, because he never once had to ask, "Now, where were we?" after hanging up the phone from one of his secondary conversations.

These types of constant interruptions and seemingly flagrant disregard for patient confidentiality are something the French are used to; however, I was shocked. "But what's the big deal?" said one French friend. "The person listening doesn't know who is on the other end of the telephone line. Your privacy is protected." Nevertheless, I made a mental note to never call Dr. Mellerio during office hours.

Living in France thus far, my life had been a series of what I like to call "we're not in Kansas anymore" moments—moments when you come face-to-face with the reality that they do things differently in Europe. Much differently. During that first obstetric appointment, I came face-to-face with the following harsh reality: completely nude medical exams.

Having recorded all the important details, Dr. Mellerio said he needed to examine me and directed me to a small room located in the back corner of his office. It contained an examination table, a sink, and a scale. He then opened the door to a tiny bathroom where I was supposed to disrobe in preparation for the examination. As I disrobed and hung my dress on the hook on the wall, I searched for an examination gown to put on, then realized with horror that there wasn't one! It was at this point that I remembered an American friend had warned me that the French do not bother with gowns during medical exams.

However, I was not prepared for the next surprise. Upon exiting the bathroom and climbing upon the examination table, I realized that there was no drape with which to cover my lower extremities. I scanned the room, certain that there had been some mistake. As I was about to hop down from the table and begin searching in the cabinets for something, *anything*, to cover myself with, in walked Dr. Mellerio.

"Are we ready?" he said with a smile.

"Uhhh…," I stammered, naked, trying to find the right words in French. "*Je n'ai pas de…*"

Dr. Mellerio looked at me expectantly, a puzzled expression on his face. "*De quoi?*" he asked.

"Uhhh…*rien*," I said, defeated. *Good grief*, I thought to myself, *am I about to go through an examination completely nude?*

I was so horrified that I remember very little of what the doctor said during the exam. Then, I beat myself up about my reaction all the way home. *This is Europe*, I told myself. *Nudity means nothing to these people* (as evidenced by the numerous topless women shown on TV selling everything from dishwashers to string beans). If only it meant nothing to me. Before every visit I tried to convince myself that I was okay with the no-drape issue;

however, every time I was on that table I found myself wishing for a bit more coverage.

However, my apprehension over the fact that I was completely nude during exams soon became a secondary concern. Just when I thought things could not get any more shocking, they did. My second physical exam started out much the same way, except this time I wore a two-piece outfit, allowing me to keep my top on during the exam. I actually felt rather relaxed having a little bit of my modesty preserved in this way. Relaxed, that is, up until the end of the exam, when Dr. Mellerio said, "Squeeze my finger."

"Uhhh…" Again I began stuttering in French. "*Pardon?*" I finally managed.

"Squeeze my finger," he repeated again.

I was horror struck. Was this man asking me to do what I thought he was asking me to do? "*Mais, je…je—*" I stammered away in French, not knowing how to put into words the absolute horror I was feeling.

He, however, seemed to know exactly what I was thinking and said, "I know this is not something that you are asked to do in the United States; however, you must try. It is very important that I assess your ability to do this."

I'm not sure whether it was the way he said it or the serious, businesslike look on his face that convinced me, but I was able for a moment to put aside my feelings of utter horror and attempt this bizarre request.

"Ugh," he groaned, "*zéro!*" And with that he turned and walked out of the exam room.

I sat up on the exam table, feeling totally exploited and yet, at the same time, a little bit insulted. Had I just been given a *score*? Although I wasn't familiar with this particular rating system, I was pretty sure that zero was not a favorable result. I dressed quickly and sprinted out of the exam room to find him seated at his desk, scribbling furiously in my file. "American doctors just do not stress the importance of these exercises," he said, not even looking up from his desk at me.

"Do you mean Kegel exercises?"

"Yes, yes," he said, continuing to scribble. "The problem is, no one knows how to do them correctly, and unless you know how to do them correctly, you might as well not do them at all," he said, a stern look on his face.

I was dying to know what the *zéro* meant. Certainly he was going to tell me; he wasn't going to leave me wondering, was he? "Why," I began, hesitantly, "why did you say I was a zero?"

"I rate my patients on how tightly they can squeeze my finger," he said, holding up his forefinger. "It gives me an idea of what condition they were in before the birth of their baby, so that after the baby arrives I know how far they need to go in order to get back there. And on a scale from one to ten, *madame*, you are a *zéro!*" He made a circle with his thumb and forefinger for emphasis. "Well, no matter," he said shuffling the papers on his desk, "we'll worry about all that after the arrival of *le bébé.*"

It was at this point during the visit that I was allowed to ask questions. I say "allowed" because the way it works in France is this: the patient is not supposed to talk during the exam. You are supposed to answer the questions the doctor asks of you, but you are not allowed to ask him or her a question. You are supposed to wait to ask questions until the end of the visit. If you can remember them, that is! Visits to my daughter's pediatrician were especially challenging since I was expected to make mental notes of all the facts and figures the doctor rattled off while examining my child. He would weigh her and measure her, all the while making small talk with me; then ten minutes later when he sat down at his desk to record the information in her file, he would quiz me on every fact and figure he had casually tossed out during our conversation. The first time this happened I was dumbstruck. I had been too busy concentrating on not speaking during the exam to pay attention to what he was saying. After that I always kept a piece of scrap paper and a pen concealed in my hand so I could jot down the pertinent info while he examined my child.

"What about prenatal vitamins?" I asked.

"Not needed," he said.

"Really?" I asked. "They give them to all pregnant women in the United States. I mean, if they aren't necessary, why do they give them out?"

"The baby gets all the nutrients it needs from the food you eat," he said authoritatively.

Yeah, I thought, *if you assume I'm always eating a balanced meal.* "What about foods to avoid?" I asked.

"I can't think of anything that should be avoided," he answered.

"Not even alcohol?" I asked.

At this, a broad smile came across his face. "One glass of wine per day," he admonished, "just one. But make sure it is *un bon Bordeaux.*"

I nearly burst out laughing. Was he serious? Not only was my physician telling me I could drink alcohol during my pregnancy, he was giving me a recommendation on exactly what to consume? He saw the surprised expression on my face and grabbed the photograph of his children from across the desk. Pointing at the smiling faces of his four children, he said, "All four, *un bon Bordeaux.*"

And with that he walked me from his office out to the reception desk. He shook my hand, another very strange and formal custom I was not used to, and said, "Here is my card." He handed me a large, index-sized card. "If you have a question about anything, call this number at the bottom," he said indicating a beeper number, "and I will call you back within fifteen minutes."

"But what if I simply need—" I started, but I didn't get a chance to finish; he cut me off.

"No matter what it is about, any question you have, call me. Day or night." This policy made me wonder again how on earth the man got any work—or sleep— done. I mean, if patients were advised to call him any-time, with any question at all, he must spend a lot of time on the phone.

My final point of contention with my French obste-trician was my weight. From the very first kilo, Dr. Mel-lerio was obsessed with how much weight I was gaining and the rate at which I was gaining it. I dreaded step-ping on that scale every time and seeing what numbers appeared. At the end of each and every appointment he would tell me that I was gaining too much too fast or that I'd never be able to lose the weight after the baby was born.

After several months of this, I decided to conduct a little experiment. I wrote down my weight in kilos so that once I got home I could look up exactly what it was in pounds. I then rummaged through a box of books where I came across my journal from my first pregnancy. In it I had dutifully recorded my weight every week while I was pregnant with my first child. I was amazed when I realized that I currently weighed two pounds *less* than I had at that very same point in my first pregnancy. Here I was, worried that I had gained an unhealthy amount of weight, only to find out I was well within "normal" range (by American obstetric standards, anyway).

"Well," I said to myself, "that does it!" No longer would I let myself feel like a failure when I heard him groan disapprovingly from his desk after hearing my "kilo count," as I began to call it. Since the scale was in the exam room, he would advise me to undress, get on the scale, and yell out my weight to him so he could record it in my file before coming in to examine me. But Dr. Mellerio was never present for the kilo count, and this gave me an idea. I decided that from now on I would figure out just how much I was going to weigh *before* each appointment. Every week I wrote down the weight I had given him. I would then return home, add a very conservative amount of grams to it, and just before my next appointment, I would write that weight on the palm of my hand. At the appointment while I was supposed to be standing on the scale reading off my "new" weight, I was instead standing *next* to the scale reading off what I had written on my palm. *Take that, you kilo obsessed* freak, I thought to myself as I read off the bogus total.

Dr. Mellerio was overjoyed. "*Très bien,*" he said upon entering the exam room, "that is a very good amount of weight to gain. Let's continue like that."

"*Pas de problème,*" I said with a smile.

His obsessive behavior regarding my weight made it all the more sweet when I returned for my six-week post-partum visit having lost every single gram I'd gained. This time I didn't need to write anything on my hand. I proudly read off the numbers as I stood on the scale for the first time in six months. "*Bravo, madame!*" he exclaimed upon entering the exam room, "you've lost ten kilos."

"I told you I would lose it all," I chastised him.

"And so you did," he conceded, "and so you did. *Donc,* let's see how things are healing."

A few minutes later, Dr. Mellerio pronounced me one hundred percent recovered. "It is as if nothing happened," he said approvingly. Of course, the end of the exam also meant the dreaded "squeeze my finger" test was coming next. Unfortunately, my score was no better than before my daughter Evelyn's birth. "Ah, well," he said with a shrug, "at least we haven't lost any ground."

This time, at the "debriefing" that followed the physical exam, he handed me a business card. "I'm sending you to a physical therapist," he said, "someone who will teach you exercises to strengthen your pelvic floor.

I looked down at the card in my hand. It read, *Dominique Le Grand, Kinésithérapeute, Rééducation du Périnée.*

"That is the person who will be in charge of bettering your score," he said matter-of-factly.

Dominique being one of those names in French that could belong to either a man or a woman, I felt compelled to ask, "This is a woman, *oui?*"

He smiled broadly. "*Oui.*"

"That's good," I said, a relieved look on my face.

"Absolutely," he agreed, "especially when engaging in this particular kind of physical therapy." And with that, he walked me out to the reception desk, shook my hand, and said good-bye.

Chapter 4
Physical Therapy for Your Hoochie

I called my new physical therapist's office the very next day to schedule an appointment. I was more than a little bit curious about exactly what kinds of exercises a physical therapist could teach me to better my score. "Only ten sessions are covered by Social Security (the French healthcare system)," the receptionist informed me. "If you need more sessions beyond those ten, you'll be responsible for payment yourself."

"Certainly," I responded.

"Oh, and don't forget to bring twenty-five euros to your first visit, to pay for your *sonde*."

"Of course," I said, having no idea what a *sonde* was.

My first session with Dominique started off innocently enough. After exchanging informal greetings and cooing over my new baby, whom I brought with me to every session, Dominique asked me to follow her to an exam room. A small desk was pushed up against the far wall, flanked by an examination table and a myriad of strange looking machines. She sat down at the desk and motioned for me to put my baby in the bouncy seat conveniently located opposite my chair. Then she opened the bottom drawer of her desk and withdrew a mobile attached to a suction cup. She stuck it up on the wall just above Evelyn's head, making her smile with delight.

Then Dominique reached into the top drawer, pulled out a manila folder, and began to scribble away in it. She questioned me regarding the details surrounding my pregnancy and delivery for nearly ten minutes. Satisfied that she had all the info she needed to treat me, she closed the folder and asked me to lie down on the table. She lifted my shirt, placed her hands on my abdomen, and asked me to gradually tighten and relax my stomach muscles. "*Très bien,*" she said replacing my shirt, "these muscles are in very good shape." She sat back down at the desk and scribbled some more in the manila folder. *Well,* I thought to myself, *that was easy enough.*

Then, turning from her seated position, Dominique asked me to take off "everything on the bottom."

"*Pardon?*" I questioned her, certain as I usually was in these situations that I had misunderstood.

"You can hang your clothes on that hook," she said, indicating a hook suspended high above my baby.

Once again, my American background betrayed me as I lay there frozen with horror, not knowing what to say or how to react to her request. Finally, I took a deep breath, got up, and walked slowly over to the corner where Evelyn sat, smiling up at me. I'd had no idea this therapy was going to involve taking off my clothes. *Okay, okay, I've been through this before,* I calmly reminded myself. As Dominique busied herself turning on and connecting all the machines, I quickly stripped and hopped back onto the table. I was then subjected to the "squeeze my finger" test, yet again.

"I felt sure Mr. Mellerio was joking when he said you were a *zéro*," she said incredulously as she scribbled away in my file. He had called to warn her I was a zero? "We have a lot of work to do," she said with a smile, "but I promise you will be as good as new when we are done!" Somehow, this comment did not instill me with confidence.

"It is very hard to learn to isolate and control the muscles we need to work on," she explained, "so I need you to close your eyes and imagine them for me."

Is she for real? I thought to myself.

"You must imagine these muscles: where they are and what they do," she continued. I had to bite my lower lip to prevent myself from giggling. I couldn't see how any physical therapy could be accomplished in this manner. "These muscles are also fragile. They tire very easily. So you will need to practice contracting these muscles several times a day for a few minutes at a time."

Now I had homework to do as well? This was getting ridiculous.

"Did you remember to bring twenty five euros for the *sonde*?" she asked.

I reached into my purse and handed over the money.

Dominique produced a small plastic bag with the image of a woman doing yoga on the front. She opened the bag and pulled out an electrical probe approximately five inches long and one inch in diameter with two long electrical cords attached to one end. She proceeded to hook up the probe to one of the many machines surrounding the table I was lying on, and then drew near to me, probe in hand.

I recoiled in horror. "What on earth is that for?" I exclaimed.

"To help you learn to control these muscles," she said, as if it were the most natural thing in the world. Clearly this was all in a day's work for her.

"There is no way you are going to..." I couldn't even finish the sentence.

"Ah, yes," she said, with a knowing smile, "*vous êtes Américaine, non?* I realize this therapy is not something that you are used to in America; however, it is essential. So many *Américaine* women get surgery to fix this problem when, if only they had access to this therapy, it could be avoided."

I sat there in stony silence, not entirely convinced.

"If you learn these exercises now," Dominique continued persuasively, "you can avoid going *pipi* in your *culotte* when you are fifty-five."

"That's not funny," I said.

"Absolutely not," she agreed. "It is not funny. But your pelvic floor has been damaged, *madame*, by the arrival of this baby." She motioned towards my still smiling daughter in the bouncer. "And if you do not fix the damage now, it will only get worse as you get older."

As I walked home, I berated myself for not having called or e-mailed one of my friends to find out exactly what exactly happens during *rééducation du périnée*. I looked at the *sonde* in my hand; it looked like some medieval torture device. Once inside my apartment, I threw it in my top dresser drawer and vowed never to go back to see Dominique. Then I immediately called a friend of mine in California who was an obstetric and gynecological nurse. "You're not going to believe what just happened to me!" I began.

Katie was certainly surprised to hear about such an unusual type of therapy, but unlike me, she was all for it. "I'd have to agree with the French on this one," she said. "That's good preventive medicine."

"You can't be serious!" I exclaimed.

"Look," she said, "Jeff stopped seeing patients altogether." Jeff was Katie's husband and an Ob/Gyn. "There's such a demand in the States for this type of surgery that he's able to limit himself to surgery only, and he's still booked five days a week! If the type of therapy you now have access to was available here, I'd sign up for it in a heartbeat."

"Well, I'm never going back," I said, "it's just too... weird."

"Just think of it as another Ob visit," Katie countered.

"Yeah, one that involves electric shock treatment in my hoochie!" I retorted.

That brought on fits of laughter from Katie. When she regained her composure, she said, "Seriously, this is a great opportunity; do *not* pass it up!"

Five days went by, and I had to make a decision. If I was going to cancel my next appointment with Dominique, I had to do it soon, lest I be charged in absentia for her "services." I was on the fence. Having access to a kind of therapy not available in the States was a certainly a positive, but did it have to be *this* kind? Why couldn't it have been something a little less invasive?

In the end I decided to continue to see Dominique. At my next appointment, in addition to the *sonde*, I was fitted with small white circles about the size of a quarter stuck on my abdomen, and hooked up to yet another machine. "What are those for?" I asked.

"Those are to make sure you do not cheat," said Dominique with a smile.

How could someone possibly cheat at this? I wondered.

"Every time you contract your muscles," she began, "a series of bars will show up on the screen. The stronger the contraction, the higher the bars will reach. Your goal is to make the bars on the top," she said, tapping the top half of the monitor for emphasis, "go up as high as possible, while at the same time making sure that the bars on the bottom do not move.

I'm doomed, I thought to myself. I hadn't practiced at home as instructed. Not even once.

"Let's go," said Dominique. "*Au travail!*"

The machine was conveniently fitted with a loud and annoying buzzer that went off every time I was supposed to contract my muscles. It went off for five seconds, then stopped and was replaced by a beeping noise for five seconds, indicating I could relax. Each "session" of contracting and then relaxing lasted only three minutes, but it seemed like an eternity. Try as I might, the only bars I could get to move were the ones indicating my abdominal muscle contraction, and that was off the chart.

From where she sat at her desk, Dominique kept her eyes trained on the monitor, and each time the machine buzzed she tried to affect my performance by saying things like, "Let's go, let's go," and "Watch the abs, watch the abs!" As if it weren't surreal enough being hooked up to an electrical device through my vagina, now I had a coach berating me on my lousy performance.

The next part of the treatment involved Dominique setting the machine up to stimulate my muscles for me. "Now you will see what it really feels like to work those muscles." What followed was one of the strangest sensations I've ever had: involuntary muscle contraction in a place where I had no idea there were muscles. After five minutes of machine-controlled contraction and relaxation, Dominique shut off the machine. It was time for my performance evaluation.

"You have not been practicing at home, as I instructed you to do," she said flatly.

"No," I admitted, "I haven't."

"If you want to make progress, you need to practice outside our sessions," she said sternly. "At least four times a day. And use this," she said, handing me back my *sonde* wrapped in its plastic bag. "No progress can be made without practice. I expect better results next week."

Practicing at home proved challenging. It wasn't easy finding a quiet moment when neither my new baby nor my toddler needed my attention. But whenever I could, I would steal away into the master bedroom for a practice session with my *sonde*. One particular afternoon, I was in such a hurry to pick up my crying baby, who had just woken up, that I left my *sonde* lying on the bed—a mistake I would soon regret.

"What the heck is this?" asked John as he stood in the kitchen doorway that evening.

I turned from the sink where I was doing the dishes to see him holding my *sonde* in his hand, the two cords dangling down past his elbow. I was so startled I nearly dropped the dish I was washing. "That...is..." I said hesitantly, "that is...for my physical therapy."

"Really?" he said in a mocking tone. "Because, you know what it looks like?"

"Yeah, I know what it looks like." I snatched it out of his hands and took off down the hallway to our bedroom. I quickly stashed the *sonde* in my dresser drawer, shut it, and turned around just in time to see him come striding into the bedroom.

"What kind of physical therapy involves something like that?" he asked.

At this point I reminded him that two weeks ago, when I began my *rééducation du périnée*, I'd tried to talk to him about what exactly went on at my therapy sessions. He was sitting in the living room, watching handball, and said, "Honey, this is a really good game. Can we talk about it another time?"

"Well, that was before I knew the therapy involved dildos!" he countered.

"It's not a dildo," I protested. "It's a probe."

He shrugged. "Call it whatever you want, but that is not normal."

He had me there. It certainly wasn't normal. Not by American standards.

"Look," I began, "I told you my Ob/Gyn recommended this therapy even before Evelyn was born, and to tell you the truth, at this point I actually think it's going to be very beneficial."

"Is that so?"

"Besides it isn't covered by our insurance." (That was an interesting conversation, trying to explain to our healthcare provider why I needed to see a physical therapist for ten weeks to teach me Kegel exercises. "But that is an individual activity, ma'am," said our insurance company representative. "After the initial session to show you the exercise, what would the therapist do for the next nine weeks?" Ha! If she only knew the answer to that question!) I continued to explain to John, "We've paid for it out of pocket. So, unless you want all that money to go to waste…"

As soon as I had uttered those words, I knew the *sonde* conversation was over. "Are you crazy?" John yelled. "How much is this costing us?"

"Well, umm…" I hesitated. Should I tell him the total cost or just the per-session cost and hope that he didn't ask how many sessions I needed? I decided to come clean. "Two hundred and seventy-five euros," I said quietly.

"Two hundred and seventy-five euros!" he repeated, his voice getting progressively louder as he repeated each word. "Do you have any idea how much that is in dollars?"

"Uhhh, no."

"That's over three hundred U.S. dollars. Three hundred dollars that won't be reimbursed," he added with emphasis on the *won't*.

I was silent for a moment. "Think of it as an investment," I said, grabbing his hand and pulling him over to sit next to me on the bed.

"An investment in what?" he asked wearily.

"In me, of course, silly!" I said. He rolled his eyes and sighed. "According to my therapist, women who complete this treatment are not only less likely to suffer postnatal incontinence, but pelvic floor exercises are also known to increase postnatal sexual performance."

"Oh, yeah? I'll be the judge of that." He grabbed me and pulled me close. Just then Carole came toddling into the room. "Papa!" she exclaimed and immediately climbed into his lap, effectively putting an end to any other plans we might have had.

"So, you never explained what that thing was doing on our bed," John said over dinner that evening.

"Well, in order to better my score, I need to practice with the *sonde* outside of the therapy sessions."

"Better your score? What does that mean?" he asked.

I then had to explain how Dr. Mellerio had given me a score of zero, how I took it as a personal affront, and how I was determined to return to him after my therapy was finished and prove him wrong. "I know you're very competitive, dear," John said kindly, "but is that really a reason to subject yourself to this bizarre treatment?"

"Look, not only did he call me a zero," I said, getting angrier by the second, "but he implied that because I am an American I would somehow fail at this endeavor. Besides, I can't let Dominique down."

My husband stopped eating in mid-bite. "Who is Dominique?"

"Dominique is my therapist," I said. "But she's more like a coach. This may sound a little crazy, but I actually feel like if I don't do well, somehow I'd be letting her down. Like her reputation as a therapist would be damaged if I failed to progress."

My husband sat there for a moment, staring at me and saying nothing. Then he slowly rose from his seat and put his dish in the sink. "Honey," he said, his voice full of sarcasm, "I cannot wait to hear how this turns out. But right now, I've got a handball game to watch." And with that, he strode off down the hallway towards the living room.

I continued to see Dominique every week, and I continued to make dismal progress—until one day, after much practice, I suddenly got the hang of it. At my next visit Dominique was thrilled with the results.

"This is *fantastique!*" she said approvingly. "We are going to show Dr. Mellerio, *non?*"

So, it was with a bit of smugness that I strode into that exam room for the final time. I anxiously awaited those three little words: "*Serre mon doigt*" (squeeze my finger).

"Wow," said Dr. Mellerio. "You've certainly made a lot of progress. I would say that you are now a six, *madame.* Very impressive indeed."

"*Mais, oui,*" I agreed, "especially for an *Américaine.*"

As I sat across from him at my debriefing, he pronounced my case officially closed. "That is," he said, "unless you plan on trying for *le petit garçon.*"

"*Non, merci,*" I said with a smile and walked out the door, thankful I would never have to return.

Chapter 5
No Cabs for Pregnant Women

One evening in mid August of 2004, I was invited to my French friend Benjamin's apartment in the Twentieth Arrondissement for a party. John stayed home to babysit Carole since the conversation at the party was likely to be at the level of advanced French speakers and my husband's French speaking abilities remained squarely in the intermediate camp. I had known Benjamin since 1997. He was an exchange student at UCLA earning a bachelor's degree at the same time that I was working on my master's degree at Cal State Fullerton. I hired him to help me with my thesis, and we became fast friends. Once we moved to Paris, he and I met up on a regular basis for lunch or to take in an art show. Benjamin and his boyfriend Olivier always knew what was hip and happening in Paris, and I jumped at every opportunity to accompany them on an outing.

This, however, was not an outing, but it was still an excellent opportunity to experience the Parisian nightlife firsthand. Benjamin and Olivier knew how to throw a party, and this one would surely prove to be one for the record books, as it was Olivier's thirtieth birthday.

Their tiny flat on the tenth floor of a huge apartment building had an amazing view of the city. Benjamin was the "chef in residence" and always served up a delectable array of *hors d'œuvers*. Olivier played the role of DJ and spun a selection of the hippest tunes this side of the Seine. Their friends, most of whom I did not know, were very welcoming but also a bit surprised to find a visibly pregnant American among the revelers.

They all asked me the same three questions: how long had I been living in Paris, what did I think of the Parisians, and did I vote for President Bush? "He doesn't seem very bright to me," confessed Elodie, a slim blond. "Whenever I see him on *la télé*, he's always repeating the same phrases over and over. Like a robot." The one thing you can always count on at any gathering of French people is that you will be asked about your views on two topics that most Americans consider it impolite to discuss: politics and religion. And you should be prepared to defend your positions on both.

Having been to many French gatherings before, and quite a few of Benjamin's parties since moving to Paris, I was not at all surprised by the line of questioning proposed by so many of the guests. Being a fairly accomplished arguer myself, I felt I could hold my own among these veterans. In fact, I got into so many interesting and heated debates that I completely lost track of time. Before I knew it, it was after one in the morning.

"Oh no! How am I going to get home? The metro is closed!"

"Just call a cab" was, of course, the suggestion offered by nearly everyone standing around me.

"Not an option," I said glumly. "No one wants a pregnant woman in their cab because they are afraid she'll go into labor and create a big mess."

The mostly twenty-something crowd was shocked.

"How can you be sure it is because you are pregnant that they pass you by?" asked Stéphanie, a pretty brunette.

"Because I've been told as much."

The fact of the matter was that John and I had been refused transport by a number of cabs since moving to Paris. Unlike their U.S. counterparts, taxi drivers in France use their own vehicles, so if the car is damaged, inside or out, they are responsible for its repair. They are also responsible for its upkeep, and many take this job very seriously. Some cover the seats with plastic (the kind that used to cover every square inch of my grandmother's sofa), some install magazine racks on the back of the seats, some even offer beverage service (for an added fee, of course). All of this came as a welcome surprise to us, since we were used to the dirty, smelly taxicabs that are standard in America. What was not a welcome surprise was the discrimination of Parisian taxi drivers when it came to their fares.

A typical situation was this: my husband and I would go out to dinner once a month. After dinner, we would exit the restaurant and immediately begin searching for a taxicab that appeared to be empty and idling. We would lean in the window and ask the driver if he was available. He'd ask us which *arrondissement* we wanted to go to, and if it was not far enough away to be worth his while (as in, the fare was less than fifteen euros) he would wave us away with his hand and close the window on our noses. This happened to us more than once.

"I feel like Danny Glover," lamented my husband (referring to actor Danny Glover's complaint that New York City cabbies were using discriminatory practices in selecting their fares). Up until I became pregnant, the only reason I had been denied entry into a cab was because I was not an expensive enough fare. Once I became visibly pregnant, I found that I could not get a cab to save my life.

I started to suspect it was due to my "condition" when I saw taxi drivers routinely slow down as they approached me, peering out the passenger side window; then, spotting my protruding belly, they would speed up and take off. I even tested the validity of my theory one rainy afternoon by hiding my bulk behind large shopping bags. Standing outside Galeries Lafayette I tried to hail a cab while balancing two large bags in front of my belly, effectively camouflaging my secret. A driver stopped, got out of the car, and opened the trunk to place my bags inside. It was when I handed them over to him that he realized I was pregnant.

"Ah, no, *madame!*" he said with disdain. "I cannot have this in my car. I just had it cleaned!"

"*S'il vous plaît, monsieur,*" I pleaded with him, "I'm not due for another three months!"

He simply waved my protestations away with his hand and placed my bags back on the sidewalk next to me before driving off in a huff.

"That is utter ridiculousness," said Benjamin, over-hearing my story. "I'm going to call you a cab right now to take you home."

"Well, you better come down with me and wait it out, because it's going to be a long night."

Five minutes later we were standing in front of Benjamin's apartment building awaiting the arrival of my cab. "We use this company every time we need a lift to the Gare du Nord," said Benjamin. "They are very reliable, you'll see." Within minutes a car outfitted with the distinctive white, lighted sign with the word *taxi* in red lettering on it drove into sight. I was standing a few feet in front of Benjamin, close to the curb. The warm weather meant I was without a jacket, and my outfit that evening was a curve hugging dress in a chic wrap style that created the unmistakable silhouette of a very pregnant woman under the glow of the streetlight. We watched the cab slowly approach the curb, and then quite suddenly speed up and drive right past us and out of sight down the street.

"See," I said haughtily, "I told you so."

"That was odd," remarked Benjamin. "I'm going to call another one."

Cab number two arrived ten minutes later. This guy actually stopped in front of us and rolled down the window.

"*Bonsoir*, where to?"

"The Eighth," I said approaching the window.

"Hold it, hold it, when are you due?"

"October," I replied. He immediately rolled up the window and drove off.

"Late October!" I shouted after his retreating tail-lights.

At this point, Benjamin was finally convinced that what I had said was true: Parisian cab drivers did not want visibly pregnant women in their cabs.

"Stand over here," he instructed, motioning me to stand to the side and a bit behind his right shoulder, thus hiding my bulk from approaching vehicles. "And let me do the talking this time," he said as another cab came into view. This one was a sleek black Mercedes. The cab driver pulled up to the curb and rolled down the passenger side window.

"*Bonsoir*," he said.

"*Bonsoir*," we replied in unison.

"Where are we off to this evening, ladies and gentlemen?"

"The Eighth," said Benjamin.

"Address?"

"Fifty…," Benjamin hesitated.

"Fifty-two boulevard Malesherbes," I chimed in.

"Okay, get in," said the taxi driver. I heard the soft click of the passenger side door being unlocked.

"Actually," said Benjamin, "it's just for *madame*."

"*Ah, bon?*" said the cabby.

As Benjamin leaned over to open the passenger side door for me, the full bulk of my body was finally revealed.

"*Mais, non!*" shouted the cabby. "She's preggers! And she looks like she's about to pop!"

"But, she isn't due until Christmas!" lied Benjamin. Then, turning to me he said, "Right?"

"Yes, yes!" I said enthusiastically. "Christmas."

"I don't care!" shot back the cabby. "These seats are covered with real leather, you see, very nice leather."

We heard the automatic door lock go *click*, and he began to roll up the passenger side window.

"Wait, wait!" pleaded Benjamin. "How about if I gave her something to sit on?"

"Like what?" said the cabby.

We looked at each other. I had nothing else with me but a small purse just large enough for my ID, metro tickets, and keys. Returning to the apartment for a something to line the seat with was not an option, as we both knew the taxi would not be there when we returned. Having failed twice before at securing a cab, we were desperate. I glanced at my watch; it was nearly two in the morning. Benjamin looked at me, then back at the stern-faced cabby, and began unbuttoning his shirt.

"What are you doing?" I whispered.

"I'm getting you a ride home." He removed his shirt and handed it to me. "How's that?" he said to the cabby. "She can sit on my shirt, and it will protect your leather seats."

"It's just a cotton shirt," sniffed the cabby. "That's not much protection."

Suddenly the front door of the apartment building opened, and Olivier came jogging over to us.

"What the heck is going on?" he exclaimed. "You've been down here forever."

Benjamin turned to Olivier and whispered, "How much money do you have on you?"

Clearly unfazed by the sight of his shirtless boyfriend, Olivier pulled out his wallet and looked inside.

"Forty, no wait, fifty euros."

"Give it to me."

"Huh?"

"Just give it to me."

Benjamin then took out his wallet and began pulling out euro bills in all different sizes. It finally dawned on me what was happening: Benjamin was going to offer the cabby a *bribe*. Of course, he wouldn't call it a bribe; he'd have to call it something else because saying it was a bribe would be insulting to the cabby.

"How about if we offered you some more protection for your leather seats?" he asked.

"What kind of protection?" asked the cabby, clearly intrigued.

"*Une caution* (a security deposit). If something should happen while *madame* is in your car, how much do you think it would cost to refurbish these seats?"

The cabby was silent for a moment as he pondered the question. "Two hundred euros" was his response.

"Two hundred euros!" I exclaimed.

Benjamin shushed me. "How about a hundred and fifty?"

The cabby went silent again as he eyed my belly suspiciously. Realizing I was under scrutiny, I tried to suck in my gut as much as I could to make it look smaller.

"Okay, get in."

"Now, just to be clear," said Benjamin as he handed over the cash. "This is a security deposit. Should anything happen on the trip to damage the inside of your car, you can keep the one hundred and fifty euros to repair the damage. However, if *madame* leaves your car in the same condition it is in right now, she will expect to receive the security deposit back."

"Of course," said the cabby politely.

We exchanged *bisous* (that French cheek kissing thing that Americans just don't get) before I gingerly climbed into the back seat and sat down on Benjamin's light blue Brooks Brothers shirt.

"I'm sorry about this," I said.

"He never wears that shirt anyways," Olivier said kindly.

"Call me tomorrow," said Benjamin, as we pulled away from the curb.

The ride across Paris to my apartment in the Eighth was uneventful. My cabby, the Rip-Off Artist, bobbed his head along to the beat of some annoying French reggae music he had blaring from the radio. I sat silently fuming in the back seat ready to give him the evil eye, but he did not turn around even once to check on me. To make matters worse, I desperately needed to pee. For a brief moment, I contemplated peeing on his precious leather seats, but I didn't want to ruin Benjamin's shirt.

When we finally pulled up in front of my apartment building, I hoisted myself out of the seat and exited the cab as fast as I could. I then walked towards the front of the car and leaned in the passenger side window to glance at the fare meter. With the added *supplément de nuit* (the bogus five-euro fee cabbies add to fares they pick up between ten at night and six in the morning) the fare for driving me home came to thirty euros. I watched the cabby pull out the money Benjamin had given him and extricate several bills from it. He rolled the rest into a wad and handed it to me out the open window. He then turned his keys in the ignition to start the car.

"*Attendez, monsieur.*" I carefully counted the cash in my hand and quickly realized that the Rip-Off Artist had shortchanged me twenty euros. "There are twenty euros missing!"

"It's not missing, *madame*," the cabby explained. "It's a *pourboire.*"

A tip? Was he serious? "My friends had to bribe you to take me on as a fare. You don't deserve a tip!"

"You should be grateful I allowed you in my cab at all in your condition, *madame*," he said matter-of-factly. "Good luck getting a cab from now until whenever *le bébé* shows up."

And with that, he sped off.

The next day, after a nice twelve-hour rest, I called Benjamin to give him the bad news.

"How's my shirt?" he joked.

"Benjamin," I said in a serious tone, "I'm afraid I have some bad news."

"What?"

"The fare was thirty euros, but the cabby helped himself to an additional twenty euros as a tip."

"Is that all?" Benjamin said, sounding surprised.

"You're obviously not upset by this revelation."

"I figured that guy would keep at least thirty euros for his 'trouble,' so twenty missing is actually quite good news."

"I'm going to reimburse you the entire fifty euros."

"Don't be ridiculous. You can buy lunch next week and we'll call it even."

I hung up feeling relieved, but at the same time I wondered how I was going to get around Paris the next few months without the use of taxicabs.

Chapter 6
The Ritz Hospital

At two thirty in the morning on a Thursday in early October, I awoke with a dull pain in my abdomen. I was thirty-eight weeks pregnant with my second child, so aches and pains were nothing new to me. But this pain was different. I rolled onto my other side and tried to get back to sleep but was awakened twenty minutes later by the same pain. Suddenly, a realization hit me: could these be labor pains? My first child had been an induction (I was nine agonizing days overdue), so I had never experienced "real" labor before.

I decided to spend the next sixteen minutes watching the clock to see if it happened again. When I felt the next throbbing pain exactly sixteen minutes later, I knew something was definitely up. I reached over and poked my husband in the ribs. He did not respond. I poked him again, this time even harder. Still, I got no response. I raised my gigantic belly out of bed, leaned over, and yelled directly into his ear.

"John!"

He awakened with a start. "What's going on?" he said sleepily.

"I think I'm in labor," I said. "I've got this throbbing pain, here, in my abdomen," I pointed to my lower belly, "and it keeps coming back every twenty minutes."

"It's probably just gas pains from something you ate," he concluded. "Go back to sleep."

"Gas pains that come exactly twenty minutes apart?" I responded sarcastically. But it was too late. He had turned over and was already fast asleep.

I lay back down again. Maybe he was right. As I lay there trying to remember exactly what I had eaten for dinner, a wave of nausea swept over me. I leapt to my feet and ran full speed to the bathroom, knocking over the nightstand in the process. I made it just in time to vomit the entire contents of my stomach into the tub. Yes, the tub, because, our bathroom, like most French bathrooms, did not contain a toilet. Whoever designed the first French bathroom decided that toilets should not be in the same location as the bathtub and the sink. So while there was technically a bathroom in our bedroom, it did not contain the equipment that most people needed in the middle of the night.

The crash of the nightstand and lamp as they hit the floor woke John again. He came into the bathroom just as I finished brushing my teeth. "Oh, honey," he said sympathetically, "are you sick?"

"I told you before, I'm in labor," I said angrily.

"Labor makes you vomit?" he asked.

"I've got to call the doctor," I said, pushing past him and reaching for the phone on the only nightstand still upright.

John protested, "Alison, it's three o'clock in the morning. Do you really think your doctor will appreciate you calling him to tell him you've got the flu?"

"It—is—not—the—flu!" I said, with slow and steady emphasis on each word.

"You don't know that for sure," he said as he placed the phone back on its cradle. "Why not wait at least a few more hours before calling him, until we're sure?"

I stood there, silently fuming, not knowing what to do.

"How are you feeling now?" John said, approaching me and placing a hand on my protruding belly. "Better?"

Truth be told, I did feel better after having thrown up my dinner. And the pain in my side seemed to have subsided. "All right," I said, defeated, "but just three more hours. I'm calling at six o'clock on the dot." And with that, I climbed back into bed and rolled over onto my side. Seconds later, John was in bed next to me, leaning over and speaking directly to my belly. "It's too early for you to come out, girlfriend," he said softly. "Stay in there; you're not done yet!" This made me giggle. The last thing I remember as I fell asleep was him gently rubbing my lower back.

A searing pain in my belly woke me out of a deep sleep at exactly 6:34 a.m. "Oh my God!" I exclaimed, trying to catch my breath. Once the contraction was over, I leaned over and pummeled my husband's back with my fists. John jumped out of bed yelling, "What is going on?"

"I'm definitely, *definitely*, in labor," I shrieked as I got out of bed and began to get dressed. "Go get Carole out of bed and get her breakfast. I'm calling the midwife." As I waited on hold for the midwife to take my

call, I silently cursed myself for not having a bag packed
and ready for the hospital. When someone finally picked
up the line, I had been on hold for approximately five
minutes and I was nearly hysterical. "Help, I'm in labor!"
I said, frantically.

"*Bonjour, madame,*" said the midwife coolly, remind-
ing me yet again that no matter how urgent the situation is, one must never forget to say "bonjour" before
addressing someone.

"*Bonjour, bonjour!*" I said quickly, in an effort to
move things along.

"How many weeks pregnant are you, *madame?*"

"Thirty-eight."

"And how many babies have we had so far?"

"Just one," I said, gritting my teeth in anticipation
of the contraction that would soon be upon me.

"And how far apart are the contractions?"

"About fifteen minutes."

"Well," she said thoughtfully, "you probably have
plenty of time, but if you are uncomfortable—"

I hung up the phone without even saying "*au-revoir*"
and sprinted down the hall.

When I arrived in the kitchen doorway I was struck
by a most horrific sight: my husband was sitting at the
table, a huge breakfast spread out before him, calmly
reading the paper. In addition, my two-year-old child
was sitting in her high chair *still* wearing her pajamas! I
stood there, unnoticed by either husband or child, for a
full five seconds.

Finally I screamed, "What the *hell* are you doing?"
so loud, my husband leapt out of his chair. "Are you *cra-*

zy?" I continued. "What is all this?" I gestured to the table full of breakfast food. "I am in labor! Get up, get that child dressed, and drive me to the hospital *now!*"

John hurried to get Carole out of her high chair harness. "I-I-I thought I had more time," he stuttered. I hurried back down the hall to Carole's bedroom and began yanking clothes out of the drawers and throwing them on the floor. "Dress her and meet me at the front door," I instructed him as he entered the room.

By the time we had retrieved the car from the garage, buckled everyone in, and headed to the hospital, it was the height of Paris rush hour traffic. It seemed like every single light we met turned red on our short, five-mile drive to the hospital. Every time John slowed down for an approaching red light, I screamed at him with renewed vigor, "Run that damn light!"

"Now dear," he said calmly, "I realize you are in pain, but I know that you would never want me to jeopardize our safety, or that of our unborn child, by running red lights."

"Yes, I would!" I shouted back at him. I tried to remain calm as contraction after contraction hit me, but as I watched the traffic move by at an agonizingly slow pace, I started to panic. I began to have visions of giving birth on the Champs-Élysées surrounded by a bunch of Japanese tourists taking my picture.

I closed my eyes and tried to remember my breathing exercises as we crawled along the boulevard. "Oh my God, this is not happening!" I lamented.

"Look, we're almost there," said my husband excitedly, "just two more lights."

After what seemed like an eternity, we pulled into the emergency room bay of the hospital. Two nurses came out and helped me out of the car, and an orderly brought out a wheelchair. I was whisked up to the maternity ward and into a large room with walls painted pink and blue. The midwife immediately came in to examine me.

"Well, you are already three centimeters dilated. I'd better call your doctor," she said, heading for the door.

"But he said it was too early," I exclaimed, the panic evident in my voice.

She turned around to face me again. "Who said it was too early?"

"My husband," I responded.

"Is he a doctor?" she asked.

"No, but he thinks he is," I said sarcastically.

"Well, he is wrong, *madame.* This baby is for today." And with that, she hurriedly left the room.

Within five minutes a doctor I had never seen before strolled in the room, accompanied by two nurses. "*Bonjour,*" he said, pleasantly. "I am Dr. Seror." Even though I had never laid eyes on him before, his name sounded familiar to me.

"Are you an anesthesiologist?" I asked.

"*Oui,*" he responded without looking up from the massive pile of paperwork he was organizing.

"I have an appointment with you today at four o'clock that I'm going to need to cancel," I said.

"I figured as much," he responded. "Well, shall we get you into the delivery room so I can give you your epidural?"

"An epidural?" I said, confused.

"You don't want an epidural?" he asked.

"*Non*, I mean, *oui*," I said hesitantly, "but I thought I needed to wait."

"Wait for what?" he said, puzzled.

"Uhhh…nothing" I shook my head. "Sounds terrific, let's go."

My first child was born in the United States, and the rule of thumb for obstetricians there seems to be that the patient has to be at least four centimeters dilated before they'll give you anything for the pain. Quite a few friends had told me that the French played fast and loose with painkillers. It seemed they were more than happy to medicate you immediately and extensively for as long as you wanted, and that suited me just fine. My philosophy on childbirth is simply this: if the end result is the same, why wouldn't you get the drugs?

I was moved into the delivery room where I received an IV of a wonderfully numbing painkiller. Within minutes my obstetrician Dr. Mellerio arrived.

"*Bonjour, madame*," he said brightly. "*Le bébé* is anxious to make her appearance, *non?*"

"*Oui*," I agreed.

"Well, let's see where we are at." As he examined me, my husband, dressed head to toe in green scrubs, came into the delivery room and stood next to me.

"There's someone here who wants to say hello," he said. I looked over to see Carole come toddling into the room. Because the French are so strict about preserving the *hygiénique* conditions in the delivery room, she, too, was dressed head to toe in green scrubs. She was so small that they had only given her the top half of a set of scrubs to wear. It looked like a dress on her and reached nearly to the floor. They'd even found little paper booties to cover her shoes!

"Carole would like a hug and a kiss from her *maman* before she leaves," said John as he lifted her up to me.

"Before she leaves?" questioned my obstetrician.

"My husband is going to return home and drop Carole off with her babysitter," I explained.

"How long will that take?"

"Probably twenty minutes," John responded.

"Well," Dr. Mellerio said hesitantly, "if you want to be here for this baby's arrival, you must return quickly."

A half hour later, John still had not returned. "*Madame*, I fear your husband will not make it."

"Oh, no!" I said, frantically, "he has to be here!" Doctor Mellerio reached into his bag and pulled out his cell phone. "Call him," he said, handing it to me. This was truly surreal. Here I was in the delivery room, my legs in stirrups, and my doctor was handing me his cell phone so I could make a call. I was so anxious I couldn't even remember my husband's cell phone number, so I called our home phone number instead.

Our babysitter Rowina answered the phone. "Rowina," I said, in a panicked voice, "is John there?"

"Mr. John left ten minutes ago," she said. As I hung up the phone, defeated, I heard Dr. Mellerio say,

"*Le voilà!*" and turned to see my husband, once again dressed head to toe in green scrubs, come strolling into the room.

"Just in the nick of time," said Dr. Mellerio. "This little girl is anxious to meet her parents." After just two pushes, my second child arrived into the world. As they placed her on my chest, a ray of sunlight poked its way through the overcast Paris sky and landed on my beautiful little girl's face. She let out the tiniest little squeak as I stroked her thick, dark hair.

"She's gorgeous," said my husband, "just like her *maman.*"

Within moments they had whisked my daughter off to the nursery and I was moved to the maternity ward. As soon as I arrived, the floor nurse came in to greet me. She explained how everything in the room worked: the TV, telephone, bed controls, etc. And then, just before leaving, she handed me a large ivory piece of paper with a watercolor stencil of the hospital on the front. "Look over the selections and let me know what you decide," she said, glancing at her watch. "You still have a few minutes before your order is due."

Inside, in elegant script, was the day's lunch menu, with small boxes next to each item where I could check off my food selections. And what a selection it was! Appetizers included crab salad on green apple *gelée*, foie gras with mango chutney compote, and mushroom quiche with goat cheese. The main course choices were roast duck *à l'orange*, sole *meunière*, or tenderloin steak with Béarnaise sauce. As I sat there staring at the menu, my mouth began watering with anticipation.

After having seen our new daughter tucked snugly in her bassinet in the nursery, my husband finally strolled into my room. "Check this out," I said, handing him the menu. His eyes widened at the amazing culinary choices I had for lunch. Hospital food has a reputation of being just awful, but at this hospital the food was prepared by top chefs. Not really that surprising when you know exactly who the main clientele is at the American Hospital.

The American Hospital is the most expensive hospital in the Paris area. Not even the National French Healthcare System will cover the cost of a visit there. Those who choose to go to the American Hospital pay for it out of their own pocket. Thus, the only people who can afford to go there are the very rich. (Past patients include Whitney Houston and Suha Arafat, wife of the late Palestinian leader Yasser Arafat). I'd seen several French celebrities there during my many visits for my pre- and postnatal care, including Jacques Villeret (most famous for his role in *Le Dîner de cons*) just weeks before he passed away from liver failure.

Just then, the phone rang. As soon as I picked it up, a woman on the other end of the line said, "*Madame*, I need to ask you a question."

"I'll have the duck."

"*Pardon?*" she said, puzzled.

"You want my lunch order, *non?*"

"*Non, madame*," she said with a giggle, "this is the nursery."

"*Pardon*," I said, very embarrassed.

"Did you bring clothes for *mademoiselle?*"

"*Mais, non,*" I said, rather surprised, "I was told I did not have to bring any, that you provided—"

"*Bien sûr, madame,*" she interrupted me, "of course, we have clothes for *mademoiselle* to wear, but some parents, they like to bring their own clothes for *le bébé.*"

Why on earth would someone do that? I thought to myself. That question was answered later on in the afternoon when I went into the nursery to watch them give my daughter her bath.

All new mothers were invited to watch the nurses bathe their babies, presumably so we could learn correct newborn bathing techniques. And even though I considered myself an old pro at this point, I still jumped at the opportunity to observe the French nurses in action. When I entered the nursery, I was asked to don hygienic shoe coverings. As I struggled to slip the paper shoe coverings over my slippers, I noticed that there were only five newborns in the nursery, yet seven nurses were on duty. When I was finally allowed admittance, I asked the nurse if the other babies were with their mothers.

"What other babies?" she asked me.

"Do you mean that there are only five newborns *total* in this nursery?" I said incredulously.

"*Oui, madame,* only five babies so far this week. But it is only Thursday," she said with a smile.

She then led me through the nursery past four sleeping babies to my own little girl, who was awake and staring right at me. "Wait here for just a moment while I make sure everything is ready for *mademoiselle*'s bath," said the nurse. As I stood there staring into my child's bright blue eyes, I glanced over at the four other babies lying there. There were two boys and two girls, and *none* of them were wearing hospital branded clothing. In fact, these babies were not just dressed; they were dressed to the nines.

One boy was dressed head to toe in a classic Burberry Nova Check plaid, a huge B stitched on the front of his onesie; the other was dressed all in Gucci baby clothing, including tiny Gucci baby booties to cover his feet. One little girl was dressed all in pink, the Dior logo covering every square inch of her. And last, but certainly not least, was a little girl swaddled in a cashmere Louis Vuitton logo shawl. This was almost too much to believe.

As I stood there pondering the consequences of my fashion faux pas, another mother showed up to claim her child and take him to her room. Gucci baby's mommy was elegantly dressed in pink cashmere pajamas. On her perfectly manicured fingers she wore several huge diamond rings; on her wrist was a diamond studded Cartier watch. And as she left the nursery slowly pushing her son's bassinet, I noticed she was wearing four-inch Gucci stilettos. "Of course," I remarked out loud, "what else does one wear to give birth?" I wondered if she had worn those shoes in the stirrups or if they had made her take them off because they were not *hygiénique.*

Just then, a nurse tapped me on the shoulder from behind. "*Madame,* we are ready for *mademoiselle*'s bath."

Watching this woman bathe my child was an amazing experience. Evelyn started to scream as soon as they undressed her, but the moment she was immersed in that water, she stopped crying and became incredibly calm and tranquil. She seemed hypnotized by the warm water that enveloped her. After she was bathed, they slathered her with the most amazing-smelling body cream then dressed her snugly in her American Hospital Logo clothing again before handing her over to me.

We arrived back in the room to find my husband and two-year-old waiting for us. Carole ran straight over to her baby sister's bassinet and said, "Why is she in the plastic box?"

"It's not a box, honey," explained my husband. "That is a special bed they put newborns in called a bassinet." And with that, Carole lost all interest in her baby sister and instead hopped up on my bed, crawled under the covers, and announced she was going to sleep.

John was sitting in a large white leather armchair, the dinner menu in one hand and a pen in the other. "Hey," I said, snatching the menu from him, "what are you doing?"

"I'm just looking it over," he said with a smile. "I personally recommend the Free Range Chicken. And don't forget to mark off which kind of wine you'd like with your meal."

"Oh, I'll do you one better," I said, reaching into the drawer next to my nightstand and handing him a folder.

"What's this?" he asked.

"Just read it," I said.

"Veuve Clicquot Ponsardin, Nicolas Feuillante, Louis Roederer. What do these names signify?" he asked.

"Just the most expensive champagnes in France. And those numbers next to each one are the prices."

"Two hundred and fifty euros?" he exclaimed. "You can actually order a bottle of three-hundred-dollar champagne in this hospital and have it brought to your room?"

"Not only that. It's brought to you by a waiter wearing a tux."

"This place is too much," said my husband.

"It's like the Ritz of hospitals," I offered. "Wait, you'll see, my dinner will be delivered by Tuxedo Guy, too." And sure enough, at five o'clock, my dinner on a tray in his hand, in strolled a man dressed in black pants, a short white tuxedo jacket, and a black bow tie.

My husband rolled his eyes and sighed loudly. "I hope our insurance is going to pay for this because I'm betting the bill is going to be pretty expensive."

"They better pay for it, since they made us come here."

The fact of the matter was I was looking forward to giving birth at one of the many government run hospitals called *cliniques,* which were only for women giving birth. However our health insurance plan informed us that I was required to deliver at the American Hospital.

Luckily, when it came time to check out, the hospital comptroller simply asked John to sign the bill. "We have received a guarantee of payment from your insurance, *monsieur,*" she said, "so all we need is a signature."

On the ride home in the car John said, "Try guessing what the cost of a six-day stay at the Ritz Hospital was."

"In euros or dollars?" I said sarcastically.

"Euros."

"Five thousand," I guessed.

My husband stuck his thumb up in the air to indicate it was higher.

"Seven thousand," I ventured.

Again, John gave me the "thumbs up" to go higher.

"Nine thousand?" I said, getting nervous.

My husband's thumb went up again.

"Ten thousand?" I squeaked.

"Ten thousand, two hundred and thirty-three," he confirmed.

"Good God!" I said, "that's like..." My voice trailed off as I tried to calculate the exchange rate. My husband was way ahead of me, though.

"Over thirteen thousand United States dollars."

"You know what?" I said. "The rooms at the Ritz Paris go for five hundred euros a night. So, in actuality, that place is *more* expensive per night than the Ritz!"

"Well, now it's up to our insurance to take care of your tab. Let's hope they're up to the task."

Thankfully, our insurance company was true to their word and paid the bill in full. We received confirmation of this a week later when we received a package in the mail from the American Hospital. Inside was a letter and a small white box tied with a pink satin bow. The letter thanked us for our "patronage" and insisted we were welcome to come back "anytime." Inside the white box was a small, shiny silver cup with a delicate filigree border. It had "American Hospital 2004" engraved on the front in elegant script.

"What a lovely souvenir of our stay," I said.

"Absolutely," agreed John, "and it only cost thirteen thousand dollars."

Chapter 7
Alison vs. the Census Taker

In 2005 the Paris region began taking a census of the population (*enquête annuelle de recensement*). On a sunny spring day in April, I discovered a large poster affixed to the back of the door to our apartment building. It contained a photograph of a rather burly looking woman along with her name and official ID number, and informed the inhabitants of our building that she would be coming to "visit" with us in the next few weeks.

It did not, therefore, come as a surprise a week later when the doorbell rang and I peered through the peephole of my front door to find the woman whose mug shot appeared in our building's lobby. She stood clutching a mass of folders and papers to her chest, smiling expectantly into the peephole. I breathed a heavy sigh of annoyance as I balanced my cranky six-month-old baby on my hip. Now wasn't exactly the best time for a chat. As I opened the door, I prayed that she would quickly hand over the paperwork we needed to fill out and be on her way. Of course, it couldn't possibly be that simple. This was France, after all.

The minute the door opened she immediately launched into a well-rehearsed speech about who she was and why she was here, which I strained to hear over the screams of my overtired child. I tried to interrupt her more than once, but she ignored me completely. She ended her five-minute speech with the following bizarre request: "If you'd just be kind enough to let me in, we'll get started," and attempted to push her way past me and enter my home!

"*Pardon*," I said. "I'm afraid I don't understand. You are here to deliver our census, *non?*"

"Deliver?" she replied. "*Mais non!* I am here to help you complete it."

See, the French government does not trust its citizens to fill out census forms by themselves. They must have help from specially trained census takers who will sit with you for *hours*, if needed, to make sure all twenty-five pages are properly filled out.

"*Madame*, as you can see, right now is not the best time to do this," I said, motioning to my now shrieking child.

"*Bon*, when shall I come back?" she said, pulling out a pen and preparing to make a note of our appointment.

"Uhhhh…" I was at a complete loss for words. She certainly was a pushy broad, wasn't she? "Why don't you just give me the census," I suggested. "Then I can complete it at my leisure."

This elicited an angry, "*Non!*" from *Madame*. "It is against regulations," she admonished me while wagging a chubby finger in my face. "I must assist you in completing the forms." Again, she asked me, pen poised to take notes, when she could return.

I decided that honesty would be the best policy. Certainly this woman would understand reason, right? "I'm afraid I can't say when I'll be able to sit down with you and have an uninterrupted conversation lasting several hours," I said, growing annoyed. "You see, *madame*, I am a full-time mother to two small children. They require my undivided attention twenty-four hours a day."

At this, she simply scoffed, "I raised a brood of my own, five to be exact! It can be done, *madame*, don't you worry. I'll be back tomorrow at the same time. So you'd best be ready for me!" And with that, she turned around and strode off to harass our neighbors across the hall.

I stood there, dumbfounded. Who the heck did this woman think she was, speaking to me like that? I slammed our door shut with a mighty *thwack* just as *madame* was launching into her spiel for my neighbor. I then dialed up Valerie, my contact at the Embassy.

Valerie was the person I turned to for advice in situations where even my extensive knowledge of the French language could not help me make sense of what was going on. After hearing in minute detail about what had happened, she sighed heavily into the phone. "These people who are hired to take the census, they are not, how do you say, the brightest bulb in the bunch." Her poorly constructed euphemism made me giggle.

"So, is it true what she said?" I asked. "That someone has to help us fill out our census form?"

"Perhaps for French citizens," she said, "but you are not French. Did she know that?"

"Oh, yes," I assured Valerie, "I'm certain she was able to figure out at least that much."

"You know, sometimes the French get carried away."

"Really!" I responded in mock surprise.

Valerie offered, "Look, I'll make a few calls and find out exactly what the rules are regarding the census and diplomats. I'll call you back tomorrow." As I hung up the phone I silently prayed that she would call me back before Mug Shot Madame came back the next day.

Unfortunately, she did not. At precisely three o'clock the next day my doorbell rang. I peered into the peephole to discover Mug Shot Madame staring down into it. This time there was no expectant smile on her face, only an angry scowl. I hesitated in front of the door. Perhaps I could creep away quietly and pretend no one was home. Mug Shot Madame rang the bell again and in doing so woke up my sleeping child who began to wail from the next room. "I know you are in there," she said angrily. "I can hear *le bébé*."

"*Madame*," I said, through the closed door, "we are not even French. We do not have to complete the census."

"Everyone must complete the census," she thundered into the peephole. "It is the law!"

I dared not open the door out of fear she would simply muscle her way past me and pin me down like some female wrestler. Mug Shot Madame was six inches taller than me and outweighed me by at least forty pounds. I imagined her sitting on my back on the living room floor, peppering me with questions while Evelyn played nearby. Again, I repeated my request from the day before: couldn't she just leave the census in our mailbox downstairs?

This sent her over the edge. She got even closer to my door, so close to the peephole, in fact, that all I saw when I looked into it was a huge pair of lips. "*Madame,*" she said raising her voice, "either you let me in right now or I will be forced to report you to the *procureur général!*"

Now there was a noun I was unfamiliar with, and since I didn't have my French dictionary handy, the impact of her statement was totally lost on me. "Go ahead," I taunted her, "report me to the *procureur général.*" This elicited an angry *hmmph* from her, and she stormed off.

Only when I was sure she was gone for good did I race into my baby's bedroom to pick her up. Evelyn's bedroom also doubled as our office and was the place where we stored all our dictionaries. As I nursed my baby in my lap, I frantically paged through my *Petit Robert* searching for the meaning of *procureur général.* At last I found it: the *procureur général* was the main legal advisor to the government. My mind raced as I tried to come up with the American equivalent. Finally it hit me: attorney general. Uh-oh.

The phone rang and thankfully it was Valerie. "I talked to the legal department. According to them, you are not required to complete the census, although you can fill one out as a 'courtesy.'" Now that was a good one. I should fill one out as a courtesy, seeing that Mug Shot Madame had been so courteous to me. "Has she been by yet today?" Valerie asked.

I groaned into the phone. "Yes, unfortunately, she has. Valerie, she threatened to report me to the attorney general!"

This made Valerie laugh. "I'm betting the attorney general of France has better things to do with his time than chase after people who have not completed the census. Did you happen to get her card?"

"Her card?"

"It is customary for these census takers to leave a business card on the doors of those who are not home when they stop by. It has a number where they can be reached to reschedule."

"Hold on," I said, "I'll go look." Sure enough, taped to the front of my door was Mug Shot Madame's business card.

"Give me the number on the card and her ID number, and I'll contact her supervisor and explain the situation," Valerie said.

Later that evening when I relayed the day's events to my husband, he let out an exasperated sigh. "Why don't you just let her in and fill it out?" he asked.

"Let a perfect stranger into our home? Are you serious? She's probably a convicted felon; she's certainly got the disposition of one."

"Now, dear," said John in a patronizing tone, "I'm sure the French government would never allow a criminal to secure such a position."

"I am unwilling to do what this woman asks simply because of the way she treated me!" I shouted at him. John shushed me, pointing to the open kitchen door. "Besides," I whispered, "that woman creeps me out."

"Whatever." John grabbed a beer from the fridge. "I'm going to watch handball."

The next day, Valerie called to give me an update. "Well, her boss was reluctant to admit that they had no jurisdiction over diplomats," she said. "However, he did agree not to send her out to bother you again under one condition."

"What's that?" I asked.

"That you accept a copy of the census from her."

Oh, no! The idea of Mug Shot Madame darkening my doorstep even one more time made me shudder. "When would it be most convenient for her to return?" she asked.

How about never? My mind raced; it would have to be an evening appointment. That way, if things got ugly, my husband could act as back up. "Tell her to come by at six o'clock on Thursday."

At precisely six o'clock on Thursday evening, our doorbell rang. I peered through the peephole to see Mug Shot Madame, once again, standing outside my door. This time the expectant smile was back. "*Bonsoir, madame,*" she said as she handed me a thick manila envelope. "I've included my card inside, in case you change your mind," she said smugly. "Have a pleasant evening." I slammed the door on her retreating footsteps.

"She seemed nice enough," said my husband.

"That's because she thinks she's won."

I tucked the twenty-five-page census away in our file cabinet in a folder I had named "French Admin Stuff." I planned on keeping it as a souvenir and as a testament to my refusal to give in to Mug Shot Madame's bullying.

However, as I sat typing at our computer a few days later, I spied our paper shredder sitting on the floor nearby, and it gave me a very evil idea.

Later that evening, my husband strolled through the formal dining room to find me hard at work on the census. He stopped, surveyed the scene, and then said, "You changed your mind, huh?"

"Why yes," I said cheerfully, "I sure did."

Several days later, my masterpiece completed, I sat down in front of the shredder and set the dial to "quarter inch strips." I then carefully fed all twenty-five pages into it. The result was a basketful of narrow paper strips that looked like the material used to package expensive china. With the shredder bin in one hand and the manila envelope in the other, I carefully poured my completed census into the envelope and sealed it. I then sat down with Mug Shot Madame's card in hand and copied her name onto the front of the envelope in my very best printing. As I left the building that afternoon to pick up Carole at school, I made a quick detour to the post office to slip the prepaid envelope into the mail. With a smile on my face and a spring in my step, I headed off to pick up my daughter. Game, set, match: Ryan.

Chapter 8
Monsieur Hyperfric

Mug Shot Madame wasn't the only stranger who had tried to get into my apartment. In the fall of 2004, just before the birth of Evelyn, I had received a rather unusual letter in our mailbox. It said, in effect, that the building we currently lived in had been sold and would be undergoing extensive renovations in the coming months. The author of the letter graciously thanked me in advance for my "understanding" and asked if I would excuse him for any "inconvenience" these renovations might cause. As is the norm in France, the signature at the bottom of the letter was completely illegible. I stood in the entryway of our building for a full three minutes reading and rereading the letter, wondering what on earth it all meant.

I returned to my apartment later on that morning, after having collected my daily baguette from our local *boulangerie* like a good Parisian, and slipped the letter out of its envelope to examine it again. I quickly came to the realization that my French skills had not failed me and that I had in fact understood the content of the letter. What remained unclear was why it had been sent to us in the first place. Surely a letter such as this should have been sent directly to the Embassy since they were the ones who held the lease. Finally, I decided a phone call was in order and I dialed up Valerie, my reliable contact in the housing office.

She answered her phone with a cheerful "*Bonjour.*"

"*Bonjour*, Valerie," I said. "Listen, I received a rather unusual letter in my mailbox this morning and I was hoping you could help me—"

She immediately cut me off. "I know, I know, we got one, too."

"Well, why would they send such a letter to us?" I asked. "We're not even on the lease."

"It's standard procedure to send a letter to the occupants of the apartment, even if they are not the ones who hold the lease," she explained.

Anxious to show off my mastery of the letter's content, I said, "So, our building has a new owner; what exactly does this mean for us?"

"What you will notice," said Valerie, "is that the common areas—the stairs, the lobby, the foyer of the building—will all start looking a lot nicer. You know, new paint, new lighting fixtures, that sort of thing."

Well, thank God for that, I said to myself, because parts of our building were in serious disrepair. "That's great," I said enthusiastically.

"Yes, that is a good thing," Valerie agreed. "This gentleman who has purchased the building is a well-known businessman in Paris. All the buildings he buys undergo an amazing transformation before he sells them off."

Had I heard that correctly? *Sells them off?* "You don't mean..." My voice trailed off. "We're not going to have to move?" I asked, the panic evident in my voice.

"*Bien sûr que non,*" was Valerie's quick reply. "The lease on your apartment runs through 2008."

Oh, thank God!

"However," she continued, "the new owner has requested to tour your apartment, seeing that he purchased it sight unseen."

"Tour my home? What for?"

"Well, he wants to see exactly how much work needs to be done to get this apartment in saleable condition once you move out."

My head was spinning over the unusual request. The lease wasn't up for *four* years; why did he need to come and see it now?

"To that end," continued Valerie, "how about Thursday afternoon?"

I looked down at my burgeoning belly; this was just two weeks before my due date. "Look," I said earnestly, "I'm about to give birth. Is there any way we could postpone that visit for maybe a couple of months?"

"*Ah, oui,*" said Valerie, the recognition evident in her voice. "I completely forgot about *le bébé.* I'm sure it will be no problem to postpone the visit. You give me a call once you and *mademoiselle* get settled." I breathed a huge sigh of relief. "Take care and again, *félicitations,*" said Valerie.

Even if I had agreed to the tour on that Thursday, it would have to have been cancelled due to the fact that my second daughter decided that she was going to show up much earlier than expected. I was so exhausted during the two months following her birth that I could not bring myself to call to reschedule the tour. As my baby approached her six-week birthday, I secretly hoped Valerie would forget all about the tour request until we moved out in 2007. Unfortunately, I had no such luck.

Exactly six weeks to the day following Evelyn's birth, I got a phone call from a cheerful Valerie asking me once again if it would be convenient for the new owner to tour my apartment on Thursday afternoon. I reluctantly agreed. Within moments of hanging up the phone, I began making preparations for the visit. I went into my bedroom, dug deep into the armoire, pulled out my nicest pair of dress pants and a silk blouse, and laid them on the ironing table in the dining room. I then called my housecleaner and asked her if she was available to clean our apartment that Thursday morning rather than on Saturday as she usually did. I was going to need all the help I could get to ensure that our apartment looked presentable in just forty-eight hours.

In the days leading up to the tour, I did a little checking on the new owner of our building. Apparently this guy was the Donald Trump of Paris. While snooping around the company Web site, I discovered that he'd started his business in 1968 and since then had completed over four hundred renovation projects in and around Paris. Their Web site was a study in cool elegance: it featured Leonardo da Vinci-like architectural drawings and a quote from Victor Hugo.

The next day at three thirty in the afternoon, my pants and blouse freshly pressed, I stood in our foyer ready to take on the role of tour guide. When the doorbell finally rang, I ran over to the peephole to peer through it. Standing outside were two men dressed in suits. He'd brought a friend? Despite this unexpected addition, I opened the door and said a polite, "*Bonjour, messieurs,*" while motioning for them to enter our apartment.

"*Bonjour, madame,*" they responded in unison. "Thank you for allowing us to visit your home," said the better dressed of the two. Clearly this was the new owner. "This is Monsieur Patrick, from the *syndic,*" he said, motioning to his companion.

"Of course," I said, even though I had no clue what a *syndic* was.

The new owner of our building was quite a sight to behold. Never before had I been in the presence of such an affluent Parisian. His entire outfit exuded wealth: Hermès tie, Italian suit and shoes, and a luxury brand watch on his wrist. His salt-and-pepper hair was perfectly coiffed, and his skin glowed with the color of someone who had recently returned from a trip to Martinique. From that point on, he became known to me simply as Monsieur Hyperfric (roughly translated, this means Mr. Tons of Dough).

After a moment of awkward silence, I surmised that they were waiting for me to invite them in. In my best Parisian-accented French, I began to describe our apartment as I led them through it, room by room.

"*Vous parlez français,*" Monsieur Hyperfric commented, clearly surprised.

"*Mais, oui,*" I said. "I am a French teacher, or I was."

"Ahhhh," he said, knowingly. The two men entered into each room, stopping briefly to survey the scene and make a few comments about its size or general condition, before moving on. I led them into each and every room in our home except for the master bedroom, the door of which was firmly shut. We stopped briefly in front of it and I explained that my baby was asleep inside and I would really prefer that no one go in, lest they wake her up. "*Pas de problème*," said Monsieur Hyperfric. "We don't need to see every room."

"Well, I don't mean to rush you out," I said, "but I do need to collect my daughter at school in a short while."

"I understand," said Monsieur Hyperfric. "I have two little ones at home myself." That revelation surprised me, considering the guy was at least sixty years old. As we walked back towards the front door, he asked me if Carole was attending our local *maternelle*. I told him she was.

"So, she is bilingual?" he asked.

"Yes, she is."

"That is a great gift to a child," he said approvingly. "My children are bilingual as well. I speak to them in French, and my wife speaks to them in English. She is American, like you."

"Is that a fact?" I said. I could imagine what she looked like. She was probably some American model who came to Paris to strut the catwalk in *haute couture*, then had to retire at the ripe old age of thirty.

At the front door, the two gentlemen paused to thank me again for allowing them to tour my home, and then each of them handed me their business card. No sooner had I closed the door on my invited guests than

I heard Evelyn start to cry. I tossed the two cards on the table in the foyer where I kept my keys and purse and ran in to nurse her. I forgot all about the business cards until later that afternoon when I returned home from school with Carole. As I set my purse and keys on the table I saw the two cards still sitting there. I grabbed them and took them with me into the kitchen. As Carole ate her after-school snack and Evelyn sat contentedly in her bouncy chair, I sat down to give them a closer look.

Monsieur Patrick's card was nothing special, so I tossed it in the garbage can deciding that if I had no idea what a *syndic* was I doubt I'd ever need to contact him. Monsieur Hyperfric's card was casually elegant, done in black and white and embossed with his company name across the top. It contained the company address, telephone number, fax number, and Web site address. It also listed a cell phone number.

I peered closely at the card to ensure I had not read the French incorrectly. It definitely said "*portable.*" Could it be that Monsieur Hyperfric had given me a card that contained his *personal* cell phone number? Now that, could come in handy in the future, I said to myself, and tucked it away in my jewelry box.

Six months after our meeting, I discovered a letter taped to the door of the elevator in our building. It bore the logo of Monsieur Hyperfric's company and informed the inhabitants of our building that the elevator was going to be replaced and would thus be out of service from August 1 through August 31. Once again I found myself reading and rereading the letter to make sure I had understood its contents before reacting. Indeed, it did appear that we would be without the use of our building elevator for thirty-one days this coming summer.

I strode over to the bottom of the staircase and looked up. Six flights of marble stairs wound around and around seeming to disappear from sight. I then looked down at the stroller that contained my smiling baby girl. There was no way I was going to lug a baby and stroller up and down those steps every day for over a month. Not to mention the fact that Carole could barely make it up a single flight herself.

I spent the next two days staring out the window, trying to come up with a solution to my elevator problem. Suddenly, it hit me. The solution was right in front of my eyes. I retrieved Monsieur Hyperfric's business card from my jewelry box and dialed up his cell phone number. He answered with a deep "*Bonjour.*"

"*Bonjour, monsieur,*" I said politely. "This is Madame Ryan calling."

"*Madame qui?*" he asked, clearly puzzled.

"Madame Ryan," I repeated. "You toured my apartment just a few months ago? *L'Américane?*"

"*Ah, oui,*" he said, finally remembering me. "How are you, *madame?*"

"Well, to be honest, *monsieur,* I'm a bit stressed. I just found out that our building elevator will be out of order for the entire month of August."

"Yes, that's true," he said. "However, don't you leave the city in August like most Parisians?"

"I'm afraid not," I said. "Unlike the French, my husband is not entitled to five weeks of vacation in the summer." (I was tempted to add that we actually enjoyed staying in Paris in August because *all* the Parisians were gone, parking was easy to find, and there were masses of smiling, happy people on the metro). "It is going to be impossible for me to manage six flights of steps with two small children," I said, hoping to appeal to the father in him.

"I'm not sure what to tell you, Madame Ryan," he said. "The elevator needs to be replaced, and I tried to choose a timeframe that would be least disruptive to the residents."

"Well, if you'll indulge me for a few more minutes," I said, "I think I have a solution."

"I'd be happy to hear it," he said sympathetically.

"The building opposite us will have a working elevator the entire month of August, right?"

"Yes," he said, hesitantly, "but I'm not sure how that will help your situation."

"Our apartment shares a common back door with an apartment in that building that has been empty for over a year. If you would agree to lend me the keys to that apartment, I could take their elevator up to fifth floor, walk through the empty apartment, and exit out their back door and into my apartment."

Monsieur Hyperfric went silent as he considered my proposal. After what seemed like an eternity, he finally spoke.

"All right, Madame Ryan. I'll have someone from my office drop off the keys at the end of July."

I nearly screamed into the telephone. "*Merci, monsieur, merci mille fois!*"

"Have a pleasant summer, *madame*," he said and hung up.

I stood there dumbfounded, holding the telephone receiver in my hand for a full thirty seconds before hanging up. I couldn't believe he'd agreed to let me have the keys! During the four weeks following our telephone conversation, I felt as if I were walking on air. True to his word, Monsieur Hyperfric left the keys in our mailbox during the last week in July. I returned home from an outing at Parc Monceau with my children to find a small, beige manila envelope in my mailbox. Tucked inside were two bizarre looking keys.

I immediately took the elevator up to the fifth floor of the building opposite ours to make sure the keys to my "new" apartment worked.

"Where are we going?" asked Carole. "This isn't the way to our house."

"*Maman* is taking a slight detour today," I said reassuringly. "Just wait and see; you're going to like this."

The key slid right into the lock, and with a quick, quarter clockwise turn the door swung open. Before us lay an apartment that was an exact mirror image of our own. Herringbone hardwood floors and mirrored doors reflected the light that flooded the apartment through curtainless windows. A thick layer of dust coated just about every surface, but other than that the apartment appeared to be in excellent condition. My oldest daughter amused herself by running in and out of the rooms, her voice echoing in the empty apartment. I walked over to one of the windows that lined the salon. Outside was a narrow, three-foot-wide balcony surrounded by a wrought iron banister. I stepped cautiously out onto it. Six floors down, the midday Parisian traffic hummed along Malesherbes Boulevard. Holding Evelyn tightly against my chest, I slowly walked the length of the balcony, anxious to see what kind of view one would have from so high up. When I arrived at the far north corner, I noticed a wide street that ran off diagonally into the distance, creating an opening in between the rows and rows of tightly packed buildings. As my eyes travelled up this opening to the skyline, they fell upon an edifice with a very distinctive shape. I blinked. Could it be? It was. I was staring at the Eiffel Tower.

So, not only did I have the keys to an empty apartment in Paris, I had a view of the Eiffel Tower. This was too good to be true. I stepped back inside to the *salon* where Carole was busy drawing pictures in the dust on the floor.

"*Maman*," she asked me, "is this our apartment, too?"

"It is for the month of August," I said giddily. "What do you think of it?"

She was quiet for a few seconds as she surveyed the enormous, empty room, and then said, "Can we have a party here?"

What a great idea, I thought to myself.

Later that evening, when my husband returned home, the girls and I were waiting for him just inside the front door wearing party hats and holding noise-makers.

"What's all this?" he said as he hung up his jacket.

"We're having a party!" said Carole as she blew her noisemaker loudly.

John scooped her up in his arms. "Is that so?"

"And here is your present," I said, handing him the small, beige envelope I had received in our mailbox that morning.

He opened it up and found the keys inside. "What are these for?"

"I'll show you," I said. With Evelyn in the stroller and a handful of books to keep Carole occupied, we rode the elevator down to the lobby, crossed the court-yard, and entered into the lobby of the building opposite ours. Once inside the elevator I pushed the button for the fifth floor. John eyed me cautiously. "What is going on?" he asked. I simply put my index finger in front of my mouth and made a *shhh* sound to remind Carole not to spoil the surprise.

Once on the fifth floor, I strode confidently out of the elevator and up to the door of our "new" apartment. My husband watched in disbelief as the key turned in the lock and the door swung open. I ushered everyone inside and shut the door behind them.

"How on earth did you manage this?" he asked.

"I'll tell you over a glass of wine," I said. I led him onto the balcony where a small tray table and two fold-ing chairs were set up with a bottle of wine chilling in a bucket nearby. We sat down, and I related the entire tale over a glass of *sauvignon blanc*.

"I can't believe he agreed to let you have the keys," commented John. "This is quite a setup."

"And that's not all; come over here," I motioned him over to the corner with the view. He, too, was amazed to see the Eiffel tower.

"How is that possible?" I asked. "We aren't even on the Left Bank!"

"Well," he said thoughtfully, "Malesherbes Boulevard is a diagonal street, so the angle and the height of this building is somehow affording us an unobstructed view of the Eiffel Tower."

Just then, the doorbell rang. My husband turned to me and said, "Are you expecting someone?"

"Actually, I am," I said with a giggle. I opened the door to find our good friends Brian and Julie outside.

"Come on in," I said. They both looked a little stunned and cautiously came inside.

"What is this place?" asked Julie.

"This is our *other* apartment," said my husband without missing a beat. "Didn't you get one?"

This elicited a hearty chuckle from Brian. "Well, uh, no, we didn't."

"You have got to see this view," I said, motioning them towards the balcony. As we drank wine and admired the Eiffel Tower, the doorbell rang again.

My husband approached the door. "Who is it?"

"Dominos pizza," was the response.

"You ordered a pizza sent here?" Brian asked, incredulous.

"*Absolument*," I said. "What's a party without pizza?"

And so it went, for the rest of the summer. We had a dinner party nearly every night in our "new" apartment. Sometimes we invited friends over; sometimes it was just my husband and me. We brought over our portable DVD player so the girls could watch a movie while we enjoyed a romantic dinner, *à deux*, with a view of the Eiffel Tower. My favorite part of the evening, though, came after night had fallen over Paris. At that time of year it did not get dark until nine o'clock or later. I would creep back in the dark, using a flashlight to find my way to the balcony, just to watch the tower sparkle for ten minutes every hour. I relished every second of my fantastic view and was brokenhearted when September first arrived and I had to turn the keys back over to Monsieur Hyperfric.

A week after the keys were returned, I dialed up his cell phone number one last time. He was truly a nice man, and I wanted to thank him again for his generosity.

"*Bonjour,*" said the deep baritone voice I recognized immediately as his.

"*Bonjour, monsieur,* this is Madame Ryan," I began. "I just wanted to thank you again for lending me the keys to the empty apartment across the hall."

"Well, I hope it made the month of August a bit more tolerable for you."

"*Monsieur,*" I said, "you have no idea."

Chapter 9
Mommy Chic

When my daughter Carole turned three years old, we began looking at placing her in a local preschool. There were several within walking distance of our apartment. Most were private, and very expensive. We also had the option of sending her to public school since children in France can begin attending school at three years of age. Since I was determined to choose a school based on its merits rather than solely on its price tag, I toured all the nearby preschools, taking copious notes at each visit. Having carefully compiled all my data, I told my husband I was ready to discuss our options. We sat down at the kitchen table one evening after dinner with papers fanned out before us. My husband perused the paperwork for approximately five seconds before announcing our daughter would be attending the local public school.

"You didn't even look at half the information I gathered on these schools," I protested, waving a stack of papers at him.

"I looked at the tuition," he said getting up from his chair and helping himself to a beer from the fridge, "and that's all I need to know to make my decision."

"But one of them is a bilingual preschool," I lamented. "Aren't you slightly concerned about our child attending a school where only French is spoken?"

John answered that question with one of his own. "Did you see the price tag for these schools? The least expensive one will still set us back three thousand euros a year. That's over three thousand U.S. dollars!" And then, to drive his point home, he held out his two hands, palms outstretched, as if weighing something in them, and said, "Free preschool versus thirty three hundred dollars a year. Hmmm...I think we're going to go with free."

I opened my mouth to say something, but he cut me off. "I told you when we moved into this building not to get any crazy ideas. We may live in a million-dollar apartment, but we're not millionaires. We are not paying for preschool, end of discussion!" He stormed out of the kitchen.

So that was it: my child would be attending the local public school where not a single word of English was spoken. But what worried me more than that fact was the French school system's reputation for strictness and conformity. Several American friends had abruptly removed their children from their local school, saying it was "demoralizing." One friend was so traumatized by her dealings with her child's teacher that she grew teary eyed every time she talked about it. Of course, I rationalized their comments as a case of miscommunication. I spoke fluent French, so certainly the adaptation to the French school system would be a lot easier for me. At least, that's what I told myself at the time.

A spot at the local public school is available on a first come first serve basis, with registration beginning in January of that school year. I was the first person in my *arrondissement* to show up at City Hall to register my child. This did not go over well with the Public Servant in charge of registration, who apparently had not planned on having to do any work until May or June. "Aren't we the early bird?" she said with a sneer as she searched through piles of folders for the required paperwork, not even bothering to make eye contact with me. "Are you married?"

"Yes," I said cautiously, wondering what on earth that fact had to do with registering my child for preschool.

"And is your husband the father of the child you wish to register?"

Now, that question really took me by surprise. In a country where it is considered rude to ask people what they do for a living, this woman was asking me if someone *other* than my husband had fathered my child?

"As far as he knows he's her father," I said in an attempt at levity. This was met by an icy stare and silence. I quickly changed my demeanor and said very seriously, "Of course."

"Then you will both need to sign these papers," she said, laying three sheets in front of me, "and return them to me no later than March thirty-first." She then laid several thick binders in front of me and informed me that in them I would find everything I need to know about how my local *maternelle* operated. I thanked her for her assistance and trudged out the door, my arms loaded down with paperwork.

According to the information in the binder, I also had to make an appointment for an interview with the school principal. And that wasn't all. My daughter was supposed to accompany me to be interviewed as well. The entire two weeks leading up to our appointment, I worried about how it would go. Carole was a quiet and timid child. The idea of her reacting favorably to interrogation by a stranger seemed unlikely. I prayed that her admission to school did not hinge on the interview.

It turned out I need not have worried. The interview was simply a formality. The principal was required to meet with all families who had a child starting school for the first time. She asked us how long we had been living in Paris and how long we planned on staying. She wanted to know if Carole was being raised in a bilingual home and if she had any siblings. Luckily she asked only three questions of Carole, and they were simple and brief: "What is your name?" "How old are you?" and "Do you want to go to school?" Carole answered the first in a very soft voice; in response to the second question, she held up three fingers, and for the third she simply nodded her head.

I breathed a huge sigh of relief when we exited the school with the paperwork in hand that officially guaranteed my daughter a spot when school began again in September. She would be in the *Petite Section*, the youngest of the three pre-first-grade classes. She would attend four days a week, in the morning only, from eight thirty until eleven thirty. I tried to find out from the school's principal exactly how many students would be in her class; however, she declined to give an exact figure saying that it was too early to tell, as enrollment had just begun. I was advised to work with Carole over the summer on writing her name and to make sure all of her clothes from underwear to socks were labeled with her name in permanent ink. I was also given a list of supplies to pick up before school started on September third. All summer long Carole and I talked excitedly about preschool and how much fun it would be. Before we knew it, it was the day before *la rentrée*.

Every child in France returns to school in the fall on the same exact day, called *la rentrée*. It usually happens the very first week in September, and it is mass chaos. The sidewalks surrounding our local school were jam packed with families walking their children to school on the first day. As I stood outside with all the others waiting for the doors to open, I began to notice that quite a few of the mommies were staring at me. As they looked me up and down, a disapproving look came across their faces. Some even looked shocked. I began to feel very self-conscious. Did I have toothpaste on my shirt? Was my fly unzipped? Then, as the crowd began to surge towards the newly opened doors, the mommy to my immediate right looked at me and said, in a very haughty tone, "Rough night?"

In a split second, it hit me. I was seriously underdressed. As I scanned the crowd from left to right, I realized that every single mommy there was dressed to the nines. And not only were their designer clothes pressed and immaculate, but their hair and makeup were flawless as well. I did a quick survey of what I was wearing: jeans, a T-shirt, and sneakers—the standard Mommy of Two Children under Four uniform for an American mom. As I stood there clutching my child's hand, the crowd of Chic Mommies pushing past us, I realized I had just got my first lesson in Mommy Wear, Paris style.

When you are a mommy in Paris, the fashion capital of the world, you never simply throw on whatever is lying around—or whatever is most comfortable. In fact, comfort is the very *last* thing you are concerned with when choosing your outfit for the day. What you are concerned with is looking pulled together and chic at every moment. Even if you were up all night with your colicky six-month-old, or waking up every two hours to feed your four-month-old, come eight fifteen in the morning, you better be showered, coiffed, and perfectly put together, lest you suffer the consequences: the dreaded evil eye from every *single* person you come in contact with! Even the nannies will give you a dirty look should you dare to show up in jeans and a T-shirt, your hair pulled back in a scrunchie.

I began choosing my outfits each day as carefully as I had when I was working full time. The Ann Taylor wardrobe that had been gathering dust in my closet since I gave birth to Carole three years earlier was pulled out and put back into circulation. I even went so far as to buy new shoes to go with every outfit, since I had been wearing mostly flats or low heels back in the day. Flats are never part of the Parisian Mommy's wardrobe. It is high heels all the time, the higher the better. But I soon found out wearing three-inch heels all day is murder on your feet. So I started to keep a pile of casual clothes on a table in the foyer of our apartment. I always wore my business attire to drop off and pick up my daughter from school, but as soon as I got home I would kick off my heels, skirt, and suit jacket and change back into jeans, a t-shirt and slippers.

"That is so ridiculous," commented my husband one morning as he watched me try to balance our ten-month-old on my hip while wearing a pencil skirt and three-inch stilettos. "Why do you allow yourself to be pressured into dressing like these women?"

"You don't understand what it's like out there," I said. "Even our daughter's teacher gives me a dirty look if I don't show up dressed like this." He rolled his eyes at me before heading to the foyer for his jacket. "I'm serious!" I said, running after him down the hall. "You are looked upon as an unfit parent if you show up dressed…" I paused searching for the right descriptive adjective.

"Comfortably?" said John, finishing my sentence, a smirk on his face.

"Casually," I corrected him.

"If I could walk around all day in jeans, I would," he said as he exited our apartment and pushed the button to call the elevator.

"What happened to assimilating?" I reminded him, "You know, trying to fit in with our new culture?"

"I say the hell with it if it involves walking around in three-inch heels all day," he said as the elevator door shut between us. "But that's just me!" he yelled as the elevator disappeared down the shaft.

I soon found out that dressing the part of a Parisian Mommy made the other mommies treat me differently. Previously I had been met with looks of disgust or simply ignored. However, when I was dressed "appropriately," I was apparently deemed worthy of casual conversation.

And so it was, one afternoon about a month after school had started, that I was approached by a Chic Parisian Mommy and handed a small, ivory-colored envelope with my daughter's name written on the front of it in an elegant script. "*Bonjour,*" she said coolly, "I'm Raphaël's mother."

"Of course," I said with nod, at the same time thinking, *Who the heck is Raphaël?*

"Raphaël turns three years old this month," she continued, "and he would like Carole to attend his birthday party."

"Well, I'm sure she'd be delighted," I said enthusiastically.

"Mmm—," she said, in response while looking me up and down, clearly relishing the opportunity to scrutinize what I was wearing up close. I stood there, uncomfortably submitting to her critical gaze for what seemed like an hour. When her eyes finally met mine again, she simply said, "*Bon,*" turned on her three-inch Chanel heels, and walked away.

Later that afternoon, it occurred to me that Raphaël had to be one of the kids in Carole's class. But which one? There were thirty-three children in her class! No wonder the principal was reluctant to tell me how many students were enrolled this year. Thirty-three three-year-olds is a lot for one teacher to handle. Each teacher was also assigned a classroom aide who assisted him or her the entire day, but that still left a ratio of approximately seventeen children to each adult. "But they are hardly ever all there," I overheard one mommy console another as they exited the school together. "You'll

see, during the school year there is so much illness going around, usually only a third of the class shows up on
any given day." *Well*, I thought to myself, *that makes me feel*
much *better.*

Raphaël's birthday party was scheduled for a
Wednesday afternoon at the end of October. The invitation said the *fête* would last from three until six o'clock.
A three-hour party for a three-year-old? That seemed a
bit long. Plus, it would conflict with our dinnertime of
five thirty. I turned the invitation over and over again in
my hand as I contemplated what to do. I decided I would
try and gauge Carole's level of friendship with Raphaël
before calling to confirm our attendance.

"Who is Raphaël?" I asked her as she stacked blocks
in our living room.

"Raphaël is blond," she responded.

"Do you like Raphaël?" I continued.

"Raphaël," she repeated.

"Do you play with Raphaël, at school?" I prodded
her.

"Play Raphaël at school," she said contentedly.

This conversation was going nowhere. In the end I
reluctantly called to confirm our attendance at the party, speaking with someone who was clearly in the employ
of Raphaël's family. "I will tell Madame you called," she
said in polite but heavily Portuguese accented French.

This would be our first foray into the world of Parisian birthday parties, and I took great care in choosing
the outfit my daughter would wear to the party since
children were also expected to be continuously well
dressed. We arrived at Raphaël's apartment at a quarter

past three o'clock, fashionably late as one is supposed to be in Paris, and were greeted at the door by the same Portuguese domestic I had spoken to on the phone. She took our coats, and then led us into a large, elegantly decorated living room where Raphaël's mother sat on a pale blue silk upholstered couch, a Limoges china tea service set out in front of her.

She was conversing with another well-dressed Parisian Mommy I recognized from school. I could hear loud hoots and hollering coming from a long hallway that veered off to the left. Raphaël's mother rose to shake my hand and say a polite *bonjour*, and then instructed her Portuguese maid to show my daughter to the *fête*. Carole grabbed my hand, unwilling to be separated from me; thus I, too, was led down the long hallway towards the ever louder screaming and yelling of what sounded like a dozen or more children.

Upon entering the enormous dining room, I understood immediately why Carole had been extended an invitation to the party. Clearly Raphaël's mother had invited every child in the class.

I stood there, mouth agape, surveying the scene as twenty-five children ran screaming up and down the cavernous, nearly empty room. All the furniture had been removed except for a large, oblong table that held a huge pile of gifts and an enormous cake. *Who leaves twenty-five preschoolers in a room unsupervised?* I wondered. *And where are these kids' parents?*

This is the biggest difference between birthday parties in Paris and birthday parties in the United States: in Paris the parents *do not* stay for the party. Basically, the

Parisians see birthday parties as an afternoon of free childcare. They disappear for hours and are very reluctant to return. In fact, at the end of the first birthday party we hosted in Paris, we were obliged to look after three children for an hour because their parents did not show up at the appointed time to pick them up.

I noticed that Carole was one of only four girls at the party, and that the other three girls were cowering in the corner trying to avoid getting knocked down by the boys, who were running around the room trying to tackle each other. The birthday boy was out in front of the pack, his blond curls just visible beneath a pointy birthday hat. They were all screaming at the top of their lungs, which echoed loudly throughout the empty room. After fifteen minutes of watching this chaotic scene, I had had enough. Clearly there would be no adult coming in to supervise these children, and there was no way I was leaving my three-year-old in here to fend for herself. I took my thoroughly terrified daughter by the hand, and we made our way towards the door.

Suddenly, one of the little girls who had been cowering in the corner dashed across the hardwood floor to my side. She was in tears as she told me that she wanted to go home. I took her hand and led her, along with my daughter, back to the living room where Raphaël's mother and Chic Parisian Mommy were still deep in conversation.

"Leaving, already?" asked Raphaël's mother.

"Yes, I'm afraid so," I said, "and this little girl would like to go home as well."

She took one look at the red-faced little girl and asked, "What's wrong, Claire?"

"I-I-I'm afraid," stuttered Claire, between sobs. "They are playing rough in there."

"Ah, well," said Raphaël's mother, very matter-of-factly, "a boy's birthday party isn't the place for sensitive little girls."

"*Ah, non,*" agreed the other Parisian Mommy. I couldn't believe my ears. I wanted to shout at her, "If a boy's birthday party isn't the place for 'sensitive little girls' then why on earth did you invite them, you block-head?"

Claire, who continued to sob, asked that her mother be called. "Well, why don't you just sit down next to me for a bit, Claire," said Raphaël's mother in a very condescending tone, "and we'll see what we can arrange." She then signaled for her maid to bring us our coats and walked with us to the door.

"Well, we'll have to invite Raphaël over to our apartment to play sometime," I suggested, not knowing what else to say.

"That would be our pleasure," she responded facetiously with a tight-lipped smile. Although I knew right then and there that we would *never* invite Raphaël over to our apartment, nor would he ever again invite us to his.

Chapter 10
The Stepford Classroom

Unlike in the United States, where the participation of parents in the classroom is encouraged by teachers, the French discourage it. The classroom is the domain of the *maîtresse*, and she rules it with an iron fist. The classroom environment is strictly controlled, and outside influences are seen as detrimental to the children's education. I was, therefore, completely taken by surprise when Carole's teacher Patricia asked me if I would be willing to come in and talk about the American holiday of Thanksgiving. Patricia's sister lived in the United States, she explained, and she found this tradition of setting aside one day each year to give thanks "quaint." I readily agreed to share the story of Thanksgiving with the children and even showed up dressed as a pilgrim. After the story was over, I showed them how to make "hand turkeys."

Since it was only eleven in the morning, Carole's teacher said I could stay until class ended at eleven thirty. As a teacher myself, I was thrilled to have the opportunity to observe her, especially knowing how protective French teachers are of the learning environment. With all the children seated on the long, wooden benches that formed a U around the blackboard, Patricia pulled out a stack of papers and said, "Let's go over our work from yesterday."

Every single pair of eyes was trained on her as she held up the first sheet of paper, the name "Jeanne" clearly visible in the top, right hand corner. "The assignment," continued Patricia, "was to color the squares blue, the triangles yellow, and the circles red. Did Jeanne follow directions?" she asked the class.

There was a moment of silence, and then a collective "*oui*" erupted from the seated children. "*Absolument*," agreed Patricia, withdrawing a black marker from her pocket and drawing a smiley face on the paper. She then placed it on the low table next to her and held up the next sheet of paper. The author of this piece of work clearly had not followed directions, as all the shapes on the page were blue. "Did Clément follow directions?" she asked the group. This time, a chorus of voices shouted, "*Non!*" "Right again," said Patricia and drew a sad face on the paper.

I could not believe what I was seeing. I sat there with growing horror, as I observed her criticize child after child's work in front of his or her peers. What kind of a teacher would humiliate her students like that? Unfortunately, this is commonplace practice in France. Children are not counseled individually about what they have done incorrectly; errors are seen as an opportunity to educate the group. And while the practice of shaming a child in front of his or her classmates has, thankfully, long since disappeared in the United States, it is alive and well in France. The teacher even made a child who was misbehaving stand in the corner while I was there. I was tempted to ask her if she would be placing a dunce cap on his head as well, but I thought that might very well get me kicked out.

Watching this teacher in action was like watching a train wreck. I was horrified, and yet I could not make myself leave. *It couldn't possibly get any worse,* I assured myself. Boy, was I wrong. Having completed the review of yesterday's work, Patricia asked all the children to take their seats as she passed out the new assignment. Each child received a nine-by-eleven-inch sheet of paper, which was divided in half by a thick, black line. On either side of the paper was the outline of a teddy bear. The teddy bear on the right side was already colored in. The teddy bear on the left side was not. *That's odd,* I thought to myself.

While Patricia was busy surveying her students, I cautiously left my assigned spot in the back of the classroom and strolled over to my daughter's side. I knelt down next to her and quietly whispered, "What color are you going to make your bear, honey?"

"That color," she said, pointing to the already completed drawing on the right hand side of the paper. And while the bear was well done, a perfect mix of primary colors, I was surprised my daughter wanted to copy it.

"Exactly like that?" I questioned her.

"Yup!" she responded.

"But wouldn't you rather use some lovely pastels?" I suggested as I reached for the crayons and slid them towards her.

"Can't," she said, "not allowed."

"Huh?" I said, bewildered.

"It gotta look like that," she said, pointing at the Primary Colors Bear again. I surveyed the work of the other children sitting at her table. They, too, were copying the Primary Colors Bear. An icy cold chill ran through my body. I left my child's side and began to walk briskly around the classroom, my eyes fixed on the small, round tables. All the children were coloring their bear exactly like Primary Colors Bear. It was like some sort of Stepford Classroom. My heart began to beat hard in my chest. "Oh my God," I said out loud, "what is going on here?"

Suddenly, Patricia appeared at my side, "Is everything OK?" she asked.

"Umm…" I hesitated. "May I ask you a question?"

"*Bien sûr,*" she said cheerfully.

"Why are all the children coloring their bear the same way?"

"Ah," she began, "well, it is important to learn to follow directions. Some students have a harder time than others with this concept." And to illustrate her point, she leaned over the child sitting just in front of her and said, "George, what are you doing?" George had chosen to color his bear completely orange. "*C'est dommage,*" said Patricia, pulling out her black marker and drawing a huge, black X across George's orange bear. "Work that is not acceptable is *barré,*" she said matter-of-factly and continued on to the next table.

I returned home that afternoon shell-shocked. I had heard that the French school system required conformity, but I had no idea how much individuality was squashed in the process. No wonder my friends had called their children's school experience "demoralizing." *Can't decide what color to make your butterfly or your bear? No problem, you don't have to decide, we will decide for you.* I racked my brain but couldn't come up with anything positive my child might have learned from this activity.

"That's socialism," said my American friend Christine, whose two children went through the French school system. "Have you ever noticed how every single French person's handwriting looks exactly the same?" she asked. Actually, I had noticed that. "How many Americans do you know whose handwriting looks exactly the same?"

"None," I said.

She explained, "We're taught cursive handwriting in elementary school, but once you're in junior high, you're pretty much free to develop your own style. You can make your letters large and looped, you can dot your I's with smiley faces. French children continue to be instructed in cursive writing up until they are in the eleventh grade! Can you imagine?" She rolled her eyes. "Socialism is all about conformity. Everyone should be the same, right down to their handwriting!"

"I find that very disturbing," I confided to her.

"Tell me about it," she said.

At the time I thought that stifling my daughter's creativity was pretty much the worst thing that could happen to her at this school. Unfortunately, the worst was yet to come. There was a little girl in Carole's class who began to physically attack her on the playground. Every day she would return home with new scratches on her arms and even on her face! When I asked her what had happened, she simply said, "Clara-Marie." Clara-Marie was a tiny little scrap of a girl. She was shorter than Carole by a good five inches and had large, innocent looking eyes. Innocent and sweet as she appeared, I soon discovered that she was the devil incarnate.

As soon as I realized my child was being systematically beaten up, I immediately went to speak with her teacher. Carole and I sat down with Patricia after school to discuss what was going on. Was there some kind of disagreement between the two girls? I asked her. Something that might have sparked the bad blood between them? Carole insisted over and over that she had never even *played* with Clara-Marie. Not even *once*!

"How could this be that a child just decides to beat up on another child for no apparent reason?" I asked Patricia.

"Oh," she said, "Clara-Marie, she is like this. One minute she is sweet, and the next she is angry and mean." I wasn't sure what I found more disturbing, the idea that Patricia already knew about this little girl's heinous behavior or that she spoke of it so matter-of-factly.

"So," I continued, "what happens now?"

"Well," said Patricia, reflectively, "we shall have a talk with Clara-Marie and pay extra close attention to her on the playground."

That's it? I thought. *A talk with Clara-Marie? How about a talk with Clara-Marie's parents? How about suspension?* This girl had nearly scratched out my child's eyes! I could not keep myself from asking, "What happens if this behavior continues?"

"Well," said Patricia, already weary of the conversation, "let's just see what happens." I thanked her for her time and returned home, hopeful that this would be the last I would hear of Clara-Marie.

My daughter came home scratch-free for the entire month of January. But at the beginning of February, scratches began to appear on her arms again. Clara-Marie was once again after her on the playground. I asked her if she had tried running away or informing a teacher as we had suggested. She said that Clara-Marie would simply chase her or wait for the teacher to be distracted, then sneak up from behind and scratch Carole as she ran past her. I marched into her classroom the very next morning and told Patricia that Clara-Marie was again attacking my child. Patricia told me that she could sit down and talk with me about it when I picked up Carole at eleven thirty. When I went to collect my daughter that afternoon, she had a new scratch on her face. This one was so deep it had drawn blood. I was absolutely furious. I scooped her up in my arms and headed straight for the principal's office.

The office door was closed when I arrived. I pounded on it anyway, and the principal opened the door immediately, the displeasure of being disturbed evident on her face. Before she could even speak, I drew her attention to the bloody scratch down the front of Carole's face. Without a word, she ushered us into her office. She sat behind her desk, her hands folded in front of her, as I recounted in detail the harassment of my daughter over the past three months. By the time I had finished the entire tale, we were both in tears.

The principal grabbed a box of Kleenex and slid it towards me across the desk. Then she reached into a drawer and drew out a small first-aid kit and approached Carole with it. As she cleaned and disinfected my daughter's wound, she apologized, saying she thought that Carole's teacher had the situation under control.

"Clearly not," I said, bitterly.

"Yes, well," she said, choosing her words carefully, "we will be having a talk with Clara-Marie and her parents."

"Finally," I said.

Carole had stopped crying at this point and was starting to calm down. "Clara-Marie is much smaller than you," the principal remarked to Carole. "Surely, you are not afraid of Clara-Marie?" Carole shook her head up and down in the affirmative. "Oh dear," she said, "that is unfortunate."

"What is?" I asked.

"Obviously, Carole is much bigger than Clara-Marie," said the principal. "Based solely on physical size, there is no reason for Carole to be afraid of Clara-Marie. In fact," she continued, "truthfully, it should be Clara-Marie who is afraid of Carole."

What on earth is she getting at? I thought to myself.

"Of course, we will be speaking to Clara-Marie's parents," she said, kneeling next to my daughter and smiling at her. "However, it would be most effective if Carole could take care of Clara-Marie herself."

"What do you mean by 'take care of'?" I asked cautiously.

The principal walked back behind her desk and sat down. "What I am saying is if Carole gave Clara-Marie *une bonne gifle* (a good slap in the face), Clara-Marie will no longer have any hold on her."

I could scarcely believe my ears. The principal of a school was encouraging me to tell my child to hit another child? "You cannot be serious," I said. As much as I would have liked to give Clara-Marie a good slap myself, there was no way I was going to tell my daughter to give her one. Who in their right mind would want to teach a child that violence should be met by violence? Certainly not someone who is in charge of a school!

"Right now, Clara-Marie has control over Carole because Carole is afraid of her," the principal explained. "However, if we were to change the dynamic and make Clara-Marie afraid of Carole, Clara-Marie would never again bother you daughter."

"Look," I said, the color rising in my face, "if you think I'm going to tell my child to hit another child, you're crazy." I rose from my seat and took Carole by the hand. "In the United Sates, if I suggested to a parent what you are suggesting to me, I would not only lose my job, I'd lose my license to teach!"

"Well, this is France," she responded haughtily, "not the United States."

"*Madame*, I am reminded of that fact every single day. Please," I implored her, "it is your job to protect the children in this school from bullies like Clara-Marie." And with that, I stormed out the door.

Evidently, physical violence was not the only solution the principal had up her sleeve. I'll never know exactly what she said to Clara-Marie or her parents, but from that day forward, Clara-Marie never again laid a hand on my child.

Chapter 11
Playgroup Parisienne

A few months after we arrived in Paris, a brilliant dad named Brian decided to start a playgroup. He posted a note on the community events bulletin board at the Embassy inviting all stay-at-home moms (and dads) to his apartment for refreshments and some adult conversation. The American Embassy Playgroup, as it became known, was probably very similar to the playgroups going on all over America at that time with one small exception: our playgroup was taking place in the most gorgeous city in the world. Thus, a morning at playgroup became almost as much fun for the adults as it was for the kids.

While the children were oohing and ahhing over the toys, the adults were oohing and ahhing over the amazing apartment. Each week a different member of the group would volunteer to host playgroup at their home. Thus, every playgroup began with an extensive guided tour during which time we reveled in discussing the unique and unusual attributes of each other's apartments.

"Your kitchen is by far the biggest, Alison," said Megan, a professional chef, who was clearly envious.

"Kristin has a garbage chute in her kitchen! No more lugging garbage down six flights of stairs. How I would love that," I said.

"I would die for Brian's view of the Eiffel Tower," commented Kristin.

Something else that distinguished our playgroup from most of the other playgroups going on in America at that time was the refreshments on offer. No Cheerios or Lorna Doone cookies here. This was Paris, after all. Adults and kids alike devoured *croissants, pain au chocolat,* and *brioche* from the local *boulangerie.* It actually became a bit of a challenge each time one of us hosted playgroup to find a selection of patisseries that we *hadn't* tried yet. Luckily, I had a leg up in the competition since a brand new boutique *boulangerie* called Eric Kayser had just opened across the street from our apartment.

Once we had finished discussing the host's apartment and the gourmet selection of nibbles they had graciously laid out for all of us, the topic of conversation usually returned to our children—how they were adjusting to life in Paris, what milestones of development they were reaching, or which parenting book we were currently reading to help us figure them out. During this time the kids roamed free around the apartment while we all kept a watchful eye on them to make sure nobody got too close to the stairs or the giant floor-to-ceiling windows that were often left open just a crack to allow in some air. Every adult assisted in managing the group of sometimes unruly youngsters breaking up fights and making sure everyone shared the toys.

Playgroup usually lasted two hours and ended with everyone profusely thanking the host for sharing their apartment (and their toys) with us and designating a host, time, and place for the following week's gathering. Carole and I attended the Embassy Playgroup every week for the first three years we lived in Paris. It was a welcome social opportunity for me and for her, and allowed us to make some great friends with whom we still keep in touch. Often, as I walked through Parc Monceau on my way to the Embassy Playgroup, I would see Parisian *mamans* hurrying through the park, and I wondered if organized playgroups were strictly an American cultural phenomenon. It wasn't until Carole was attending our local *maternelle* four mornings a week that I had the opportunity to experience a playgroup *Parisienne.*

During the very first week of school, I was approached by a slim brunette as I buckled Evelyn back into her stroller for the trip home.

"It's quite an adjustment having one at home now, huh?" she said with a smile.

"I'm finding I have a so much free time that I'm not sure what to do with myself." I noticed she, too, had a baby in her stroller. "And who do we have here?"

"This is Julien. He's eight months. And yours?"

"Evelyn, she's ten months. My oldest, Carole, is three. She just started in *la Petite Section.*"

"My oldest, Xavier, is in the *Petite Section* as well. He's still a little sad when I drop him off, but as soon as I leave the tears disappear."

"Oh, my goodness, my daughter is doing the exact same thing. I think she's trying to make me feel guilty for leaving her at school for a whole three hours."

This elicited a hearty chuckle from her.

I introduced myself. "My name is Alison."

"I'm Claire," she said with a smile.

"Well, we'd better get going."

"You know, there is a weekly meeting organized by the *mairie* for moms like us."

"Moms like us?"

"You know, *les femmes de foyer*" (stay-at-home moms).

"Is that so? When is it?"

"Every Thursday at ten in the morning. Here, let me give you the address," she said pulling a pen and a scrap of paper from her purse. "I hope to see you there." And with that she turned and headed in the opposite direction with her son.

I looked down at the paper in my hand. The address did not look familiar. I'd have to go home and look it up in my trusty Michelin Paris Atlas. Turns out that the playgroup was not located at the nearby *mairie* after all but in a church a good thirty minutes walk from our apartment. Quite a ways to travel for an hour-long playgroup, but my curiosity about what exactly would take place at a Playgroup *Parisienne* got the best of me. I had to attend at least once.

On the following Thursday morning after dropping off Carole in her classroom, Evelyn and I began the long, uphill walk to the church in the very furthest corner of the Eighth Arrondissement. A steady wind and driving rain began to pound us as we got halfway there, which meant that by the time we arrived my freshly pressed pants were wrinkled, my shoes were muddy, and my carefully coiffed hair was disheveled.

Alas, it wouldn't have mattered anyway because the moment I stepped into the small room reserved for our meeting I knew I was, once again, woefully under-dressed. I had carefully selected my outfit that morning: a chocolate brown wool sweater and a pair of plaid wool pants. And while I would normally wear my very highest heels to any event that included Parisian Mommies, the two-mile walk this gathering entailed necessitated more practical footwear. I had decided to wear a pair of dark brown suede loafers with an elegant gold buckle across the front. I realized now that choosing comfort over style was clearly a mistake. Every single mommy there seemed to be dressed in almost identical outfits: a slim pencil skirt, a silk blouse, and sky-high stiletto heels. So, here was the first big difference between our American playgroup and the Playgroup *Parisienne*: while we American moms dressed with comfort in mind, Parisian moms always dressed with style in mind.

I paused for only a moment to reflect on my fashion faux pas before deciding that I had come this far and might as well stay regardless of the fact that I was not properly dressed. I parked my stroller next to the coat rack and leaned over to unbuckle Evelyn, placing her on the floor in front of me while I carefully shook out my soaking wet raincoat.

"Well, hello there, Alison," said a voice from behind me. I turned around to see Claire smiling back at me. "I am so glad you could make it."

"Well, we almost didn't," I said gesturing to my soaking raincoat.

"I know, it's just horrible out there today. Come on, let me introduce you around."

I picked up Evelyn and began to follow Claire over to the other side of the room where all the mommies had gathered around a small wooden table that held refreshments. There were five women standing around chatting, each holding a small paper cup. On the table in front of them was a large platter of French butter cookies and an old-style press espresso machine.

"Ladies, I'd like to introduce you to a new friend of mine. Her name is Alison."

Claire quickly went around the circle, rattling off everyone's name. "This is Catherine, Sylvie, Marie, Christine, and Isabelle."

"*Enchantée,*" I said with a smile. "And this is Evelyn, she's ten months."

"She is lovely," said Sylvie reaching out to touch Evelyn's hand. "Just look at her amazing blue eyes!"

Evelyn immediately began to reach for one of the delicious butter cookies she saw on the table. Sylvie reached down and picked up the plate, holding it up just in front of her so she could select her favorite. Once Evelyn had a cookie in hand, Claire led me over to the center of the room where a medium-sized cardboard box had been placed on the floor.

"Here is what you came for, right?" said Claire as she began to pull all sorts of toys out of the box and place them on the floor next to Evelyn.

I scanned the room of crawling babies and toddling toddlers but could not locate Claire's son.

"Where is Julien?" I asked, a bit confused.

"Oh, I left him at home with the au pair," said Claire matter-of-factly. "I needed a break."

Here was the second big difference between our American playgroup and the Playgroup *Parisienne*: some of the moms left their children at home and just came to enjoy the company of other adults! *What a great, and indulgent idea,* I thought to myself.

Once Evelyn was contentedly playing with the toys set up all around her, Claire waved me back over to the table.

"*Un café?*" she asked, proffering a small cup of steaming dark brown liquid.

"*Merci.*"

"So we were just talking about summer vacation. Where did you go this past summer?"

"Well, we spent some time in the southwest."

"Where?"

I hesitated. "I'm afraid I don't remember the name of the town."

"Was it Biarritz?" asked Catherine. "We were in Biarritz this summer."

"No, wait, sorry, I meant the south*east.*"

"Then it was Saint-Tropez, right?" said Isabelle. "Don't you hate how crowded it is now? When we first started going there, it was so unspoiled; now, well..." Her voice trailed off.

Truth be told, I remembered exactly the name of the town we had stayed in. It was called Narbonne Plage, and it was an inexpensive and very *un-trendy* town on the border of Spain and France. I was reluctant to reveal this fact to the well-heeled crowd of Parisian mommies who surrounded me, for the simple fact that chic Parisians did not vacation *anywhere* but Cannes, Saint-Tropez, or Biarritz in the summer.

In an attempt to keep from having to answer any more questions I grabbed a cookie from the platter and began to devour it. However, I needn't have worried. The conversation about everyone's fabulous summer vacation went on without me. And on and on and on. In fact, it never seemed to end. *How long could one possibly discuss a vacation?* I thought to myself.

Luckily for me, right at that moment Evelyn started to fuss, and a glance at my watch told me it was time for her to nurse. I walked over, scooped her into my arms, and carried her over to one of the many ancient-looking wooden chairs that lined the walls of the room. I was nursing quite contentedly for a few minutes when all of a sudden a small girl came over and stood in front of me. She moved in quite close and began to stare intently at my exposed breast. It was the most attention I had received from anyone while nursing since moving to Paris.

"*Bonjour,*" I said, in an attempt to distract her uncomfortable stare. "What is your name?"

"Elise," she said with a shy smile.

"Elise, my name is Alison and this is Evelyn."

The little girl gave no response and continued to stare with fascination at my nursing baby. After another two minutes of staring in silence, the girl's mother finally came over and tried to lead her away.

"Come now, Elise," she said, "let's give Alison and Evelyn a little space."

"But, *maman,* what is she doing with that baby?"

"Why, she's feeding her, of course!"

How was it possible that in this city where mothers were free to feed their babies anywhere they liked that this little girl had never witnessed a mother breast-feed her child?

"Did you feed me like that?"

"When you were little, yes, but not when you were as old as this baby."

And with that final explanation, Elise allowed herself to be led away.

This revelation did not come as a complete surprise to me. My French pediatrician, with whom I generally got along well, did raise an eyebrow when I told him that I intended to breast-feed each of my daughters for at least a year. And while he did not discourage me from doing so, he certainly did not *encourage* me, either. Yes, the irony of all ironies is that in France, where mothers are free to breast feed anywhere and everywhere, women are not encouraged to do so for more than a few weeks (even though it is the norm for American pediatricians to routinely advise their patients to breast-feed for as long as possible). Whenever I would mention that I was still breast-feeding at Evelyn's well-baby visits, my pediatrician would always act surprised and say, "*Ah, bon* are we still doing that?"

When Evelyn had finished nursing, I walked back over to the center of the room and placed her down on the carpet next to the set of blocks she had been playing with before. I returned to the group of women still gathered around the refreshment table to find that the conversation had thankfully shifted from summer vacation to a new topic: *rééducation du périnée.* Now here was a topic I did have knowledge of—but the idea of sharing my....uh...experiences with a group of women I barely knew frightened me even more than admitting we had vacationed in Narbonne Plage. It seemed everyone in the group was sharing their experiences in an attempt to help Christine find a good therapist for herself.

"I went to this great woman in the Seventeenth. I can't remember her name but I'll bring you her card next time," said Marie.

"Well, if you want to stay in the Eighth, I have a fabulous therapist whose office is right across from Monceau Fleurs," offered Catherine.

"Well, technically I'm supposed to wait until I'm six weeks postpartum, but I'm not sure I can wait that long," admitted Christine.

I could scarcely believe my ears. Christine, the thinnest and most put together woman there, was actually a brand-new mom?

"How old is your baby?" I asked, dreading the answer.

"He's almost five weeks" was her response.

I nearly dropped my espresso. A month after giving birth and she looked like *that?* There was no trace of any baby weight anywhere on her. Neither her face nor her hands were puffy, and her stomach appeared flatter than mine was when I was a seventeen-year-old. I reached for another cookie from the platter. It was at that very moment that another shocking reality hit me. I was the *only* one, besides the kids, who was eating those cookies. I had not seen a single Parisian mommy pick up even one of them. I froze in mid-chew. What to do? I knew the answer immediately: give the cookie to Evelyn. I headed over in my daughter's direction just in time to see a small boy walk up to her and smack her on the head with a drumstick.

"No, no, no!" I said, rushing over to pick up Evelyn, who was now crying. "The drumsticks are for use on the drum." I led the Head Drummer over to the tin drum that had been abandoned just a few feet away. The little boy gave no response, simply walked over to another barely mobile baby and hit him on the head with the drumstick, resulting in another crying baby.

"Hey," I said growing angry, "drumsticks are not for hitting others!"

The Head Drummer once again said nothing and strolled off in search, no doubt, of another helpless victim. This time I ran after him and grabbed the drumstick out of his hand before he could strike again.

"If you cannot play with this in the correct manner, then it's going away," I informed him.

I looked around at that point, certain that Head Drummer's mommy would be standing there waiting to discipline him (or at least back me up on what I was trying to teach him)—but alas, no. There were no other mommies *anywhere* near us. They were all still at the refreshment table discussing their hoochie physical therapy and sipping espresso.

Here was the third big difference between our American playgroup and Playgroup *Parisienne*: no one here was watching the kids. The children were left to fend for themselves, and not even the terrified screams of a hurt child could distract the adults from their very important conversation. At the American playgroup, our adult conversations were always *secondary* to the safety and well being of all the children at the playgroup. More than once during the many playgroups I attended, someone I was talking to would to dash off in mid-sentence when they saw their child, or another person's child, who needed help or needed to be disciplined. Not so at Playgroup *Parisienne*. I was the one and *only* adult who was policing the behavior of the children present. More surprising than this fact was the attitude of the mommies regarding their children's behavior. When I mentioned the offending child's bad behavior to his mother, she seemed not to be bothered by the fact that her child was routinely beating up on those younger than himself.

I discovered that the basic philosophy on childrearing in France is that parents feel that children should learn to work out their differences by *themselves*. And while I do agree that children who have reached the age of reason (five years and older) should be encouraged to solve their own quarrels, children younger than five rarely have the reasoning skills (or verbal skills) to solve their own disputes. Lack of consequences for their actions simply teaches these very young children that if they are bigger and stronger than their peers, they can do whatever to whomever, whenever they want.

Since Head Drummer's mommy showed absolutely no sign of stepping in to curb his bad behavior, I decided that Evelyn would be safer with me and carried her over to the refreshment table where she helped herself to another cookie. And just when I thought this playgroup couldn't get any more shocking, it did! I watched with growing horror as brand-new mommy Christine set her purse on the refreshment table, placed her hand inside, and withdrew a package of cigarettes and a lighter! She then pulled out a ciggy and lit up, right there in front of my ten-month-old daughter and her own four-week-old son who was parked nearby, snoozing in his stroller. As I watched Christine puffing away, I tried to imagine the reaction of the other parents at our American playgroup if I pulled out a pack of Marlboros and lit up.

It was at that point that I decided I had experienced enough Playgroup *Parisienne* and slowly made my way over to the coat rack. As I was buckling Evelyn into her stroller, Claire appeared at my side.

"Leaving already?"

"Yes, I'm afraid so. I've got some errands to run before I pick Carole up from school."

"Well, I'm so glad you could make it today, and I hope we'll see you again soon."

Claire and I became friends and had several play dates with just our two children, but unfortunately her husband was transferred by his company to Manhattan and they left Paris just two months later. I never returned to Playgroup *Parisienne*, deciding that I had very little in common with the high society Parisian Mommies that frequented it. The cultural difference in parenting styles were just too much to overcome.

Chapter 12
Au Revoir, Paris!

"Do you realize you're living the life that most people only dream about?" wrote my college advisor in an e-mail after we had first moved to Paris. "Why would you ever leave?" Well, the simple answer of course is that we *had* to leave. My husband's assignment in Paris was originally for three years, and it had already been extended once. However, a more accurate answer would be to say that we *wanted* to leave.

We knew it was time to return home when our older daughter, Carole, started to inform everyone she met that she was French. This drove my fiercely patriotic husband crazy. "No, no, no!" He would say sternly, "*Américaine*, Ah-mer-E-can." And while I admonished him for being a bit overzealous in his correction of her, I, too, was bothered by the fact that despite our best efforts, Carole seemed to feel absolutely no connection to her home country. Speaking English with her at home, reading to her in English, and watching American television shows on DVD did nothing to fill in the gap that was missing: knowledge of the American culture.

We knew living as expatriates abroad that the language, customs, and culture of our host country might exert a stronger influence on our children than our native culture, but we had no idea it was going to eclipse it. After five years in Paris, our girls identified more with

Mardi Gras than with Halloween, and with Bastille Day more than the Fourth of July. Even Thanksgiving was a mystery to them (even though we cooked a turkey every year and invited all our French friends over to participate in this uniquely American celebration). We were living in a vacuum of American culture, and the only remedy for that was to return to the United States.

On the evening of our last night in Paris, we decided to eat dinner on the Champ de Mars in the shadow of the Eiffel Tower. We packed a picnic, grabbed the last bottle of wine out of the fridge, and headed to the metro. As the cars hummed along the track, our daughters were abuzz with excitement. Finally, *maman* and *papa* had agreed to let them stay up late enough to see the twinkling lights on the Eiffel Tower. We spread out our blanket alongside the dozens of others who had come to watch the light show as well. As we ate foie gras and sipped wine from plastic cups, we watched the sun set slowly over the horizon.

The girls made friends with the nearby children and amused themselves playing games of chase for an hour after dinner. As the sky began to darken, our children returned to the comfort of the blanket and the warmth of their two parents. We sat there, all four of us, huddled together like school chums on a front porch, and let out a collective sigh when the tower finally illuminated before our eyes. We watched it light up and darken every ten minutes for a full hour before our children's bowed heads and limp arms told us it was time to go home.

As we turned to leave, each of us carrying a sleeping child, my oldest suddenly spoke up. "Where are we going?"

"We're going home," I whispered. "Wave good-bye to the Eiffel Tower; we won't be seeing it again for a while." Carole, her eyes still firmly shut, raised one of the arms she had wrapped around my husband's neck in a halfhearted wave then let it fall limply down his back.

I grew teary-eyed as I opened their bedroom window later that night, knowing it was the last time they would fall asleep listening to the noise of the Paris streets. After safely tucking them in, I retreated to the quiet of the bedroom John and I had shared for five years.

The floor was littered with boxes and rolls of packing tape. The only source of light in the room came from the sliver of a moon that shone down through the large, open window. I walked over to it feeling the soft breeze as it entered the room. As I stood looking out onto the courtyard below, warm, silent tears began to flow down my cheeks. Before I knew it, I was heaving heavy sobs that were now becoming audible. Alerted by the sound of my crying, my husband came rushing into the darkened room, stopping briefly when he saw my silhouette as I sobbed uncontrollably into my hands.

He walked up to me, placing his hands on mine and removing them from my face. "What's wrong?" he asked. "Surely you're not sad about leaving Paris?" When I didn't respond, he continued. "But, honey, you've been dying to return to the United States!"

"I know, I know," I said, choking back another sob. "It's not so much Paris as it is this place." I gestured around the room. "This apartment has been our home for the past five years. So many memories made within these walls, and now we have to leave them all behind." I began sobbing anew.

"But we'll make new memories in our next home," said John earnestly. "And we can always come back to visit."

His kind words did little to comfort me. I was distraught when I went to bed that evening, and I slept fitfully, waking up every few hours and walking around our nearly empty apartment in the dark. I ran my hands along the beautifully carved marble fireplaces and over the crown molding that covered the doors and the walls, trying to burn the images into my brain. Lots of happy memories had taken place here, and some sad ones, too. This apartment was the only tangible reminder I had of those memories; and when it was gone from my life, I was afraid they would be gone, too.

As dawn broke over our last day in Paris, I stood in the window of our living room, leaning on the ornate wrought iron railing and watching the sun slowly illuminate the blue roofs of the adjacent buildings. The nearby St. Augustin church bells tolled out the hour. How I had complained to my husband about those noisy bells when we first moved in here! The thought of this made me chuckle in spite of my sadness. Within a few minutes, I heard my girls running around the apartment, their voices echoing in the empty rooms. John made his last trip to our local *boulangerie* for *croissants* and *café*, which we enjoyed sitting on boxes in the living room.

A few hours later, as we stood in the front hall of the only home my children had ever known, my eyes filled with tears again. I went to the front door and placed my back against it, closing my eyes and imagining the way I felt that first time we opened the door to this empty apartment five long years ago: the hope, the excitement, the fear. Before I knew it, I was sobbing again.

"What is wrong with *maman*?" asked Carole.

"She's just a little sad," answered John.

"But why?"

"Because we are leaving Paris."

"But we'll come back someday, right?" asked Carole, a bit panicked.

"Yes," her father assured her, "we'll come back someday." Then he leaned close to me. "Honey," he whispered in my ear, "it's time to go."

On the ride to the airport, the girls squealed with excitement as the monuments of Paris passed by our window. Charles de Gaulle was a madhouse, as usual—too many people crammed into too small a space. Tourists were running here and there, pushing everyone out of the way in an effort to make their flight. Despite all the chaos surrounding my family and me, I remained unusually calm. I was lost in thought, trying to imagine my life without this city in it. When we finally were able to check in and unload our heavy bags onto the airline personnel, my husband heaved a huge sigh of relief. "Now all we have to lug around is four carryons and a stroller!" he said cheerfully.

When we finally boarded the plane, it was my turn to breathe a huge sigh of relief. A wave of excitement washed over me: we were going home! Unfortunately, the good feelings didn't last long. It had been five years since I had last boarded an American airline on a transatlantic flight, and in the interim the conditions had only gotten worse. Our four seats in coach had precious little leg room. Only our two young children were able to sit without having their knees touch the seat in front of them. I watched in horror as my six-foot-five husband struggled to get comfortable during the entire eight-hour flight.

As we neared Dulles airport, our ordeal nearly over, we got some bad news. A huge thunderstorm was battering Northern Virginia, and it was deemed unsafe to land at this time. The pilot informed us that we were being diverted to BWI airport. "No!" I screamed in horror. "We'll miss our connecting flight!"

John reached over and held my hand. "Don't worry, honey, it will be OK."

"No it won't!" I insisted. "If we miss our connection to the West Coast, we'll be stuck at BWI for the night!" Images of the four of us sleeping on top of a heap of suitcases in a darkened terminal flashed in my head. I began crying hysterically. "Please, God, don't let this happen to us!" I whispered.

At that exact moment, the pilot came on the intercom system once again. He informed us that we had been given permission to circle the airport for a half hour in the hopes that the winds would die down enough for us to land safely. "Keep your fingers crossed," he instructed us. Not only did I cross my fingers but also those of my two little girls as I held one of each of their hands tightly in mine.

Within ten minutes we received the news we had been praying for: the wind had died down enough for us to attempt a landing. It was a bit of a bumpy ride and not an experience I'd ever want to repeat, but when we were finally wheels down the plane erupted with deafening applause. When we reached the terminal, I stopped dead in my tracks, got down on my knees, and kissed the ground. "Now there's someone who is glad to be home," said a passerby who observed my actions.

"You have no idea."

Now all we had to do was clear customs, transfer our luggage to our connecting flight, and head for our departure gate: all in under *sixty* minutes. Our comfortable two-hour cushion between flights had now been whittled down to an hour. If we were going to make our connection, we had to move fast. I had insisted that we all wear thin-soled shoes in an effort to avoid the "shoe bomber" security checks. Unfortunately that rule had been changed, too. All footwear, no matter how thin and seemingly benign, *had* to be removed. It took us so long to make it though security that we didn't even stop to put our shoes back on after we were through. All four of us ran, shoeless, through the terminal to the luggage claim and then to the first United Airlines representative we could find. He retagged our luggage and sent it on its way, presumably to be loaded onto our connecting flight.

As the clock ticked down, we frantically searched for our departure gate in the maze of the airport. It didn't help matters that we were travelling at the height of the summer season and that the storm we had just managed to land in had stranded most of the outgoing aircraft. The lounges and hallways overflowed with stranded passengers. For the last time, we joined a seemingly unending line of passengers waiting to make it through a security checkpoint. After having finally buckled and fastened everyone's shoes back on, we were again asked to remove our footwear.

I glanced at my watch: just twenty minutes until departure. "We're not going to make it!" I whispered to my husband, who was standing just in front of me.

"Honey," he said, squeezing my hand, "don't panic."

Again I looked at my watch and then at the long line of passengers, which had not budged an inch during the last five minutes. In an instant I knew what I had to do. I dropped my carry-on bag down on the ground and folded my hands in front of me. I closed my eyes and said, out loud, "Dear God, if you allow us to make this connection, I swear to you I will never leave U.S. soil again!"

This provoked nervous laughter from most of those standing around us, except for one man. He said, "Hey, we'd like to get in on that request." I turned around to see a father, apparently traveling alone with two young children. He smiled knowingly at me. "I could use all the help I can get."

I returned his smile and said, "Absolutely!"

I folded my hands in front of me again and said, "Dear God, please include this nice gentleman and his two children in on that last request." Amazingly, as soon as I had finished my prayer, the line started to move. Two security guards had apparently returned from their dinner break and opened up several more checkpoints. The huge line of passengers quickly thinned out and within minutes we were sprinting towards our departure gate. I caught one last glimpse of that dad as he and his children ran off in the opposite direction from us after passing through security. He smiled at me and gave me the thumbs-up sign. I did the same as I mouthed the words, "Good luck."

The last flight we took on our journey home was smooth and uneventful. Our girls, who had now been awake for twenty hours straight, were exhausted. They slept the entire flight. So did my husband. I, unfortunately, could not. I was still too stressed out, worried that something would go wrong and we'd never make it to our destination. I truly could not relax until the children were safely tucked into bed at my husband's parents' house later that evening.

"Did you really mean it when you said you'd never leave U.S. soil again?" John asked me as he lay down beside me.

"Of course, I meant it!" I said. "I'm never leaving America, *ever* again!"

Chapter 13
Epilogue

There were times during our five years in Paris when I truly felt as if I were a part of the nineteen nineties television series *Lifestyles of the Rich and Famous.* We had front row seats to historic events such as Lance Armstrong's last *Tour de France* in 2005 before he retired (the first time) and made the acquaintance of more than a few famous people (like First Lady Laura Bush whom we met at a special "meet and greet" for Embassy families organized by her staff). I accompanied my husband to more than a few social gatherings where, if you weren't wearing a floor-length gown and fur stole, you felt underdressed.

While the children of my friends back in the States went on field trips to the zoo, Carole went on field trips to the Louvre. Both my daughters now possess a native accent when speaking French (an accent which still eludes me after twenty-five years of studying the language) and their passports contain more country stamps than mine and my husband's combined. And though they have only faint memories of their European travels, we have the photographs to prove it.

Our relocation team at the American Embassy warned us that our transition back to life in the United States might prove *more* difficult that our transition to life in Paris, although we did not find that to be the case. And while my husband and I occasionally experience gaps in our American pop culture knowledge, I have discovered there is an upside to missing out on the majority of American television programs from 2002 to 2007 (like *Britney and Kevin: Chaotic*). Living in Paris was an experience I will never forget, and I will be forever grateful for the opportunities it afforded my children and me. However, as Dorothy from Kansas once said, "There's no place like home."

Chapter 14
Hits and Misses

Sitting at a sidewalk café taking in views of the Seine, the Champs Élysées, or even the Eiffel Tower. Sounds magical, doesn't it? Well, it wasn't all magical. Here are a few of the things I miss (and don't miss) about living in the City of Lights.

What I miss:

1) **Doctors who make house calls.** Yes, a practice that disappeared in the United States more than fifty years ago is still alive and well in France. You simply dial up an agency called *SOS Médécins*, tell them who the patient is and what the problem is, and within an hour or so (depending on the time of day) a general practitioner will show up at your door ready to evaluate the patient. He (or she) will also write prescriptions for any medicines needed, and it all costs just fifty-five euros. This service is available twenty-four hours a day, seven days a week.

2) **My pediatrician's cell phone number**. French pediatricians give their patients their cell phone number, and while I found this practice rather odd, I quickly came to appreciate its benefits. Having a direct line to our pediatrician allowed us to avoid dragging our

sick children (with their immature immune systems) into the office where we knew there would be tons of germs waiting to pounce on them. The doctor was able to diagnose most ailments over the phone, enabling my children to receive treatment without ever having to leave the comfort of our own home! And when Carole fell off the merry-go-round at Parc Monceau and we thought she might have broken her arm, I was in touch with her doctor within *three minutes* of her accident. He instructed us to bring her to his office immediately where he was *waiting* to examine her. There is no more stressful situation for a parent than when your children are sick, or worse, injured. In this case, we found the French way of doing things much better than the American way and only wish that American pediatricians could find a way to make this model work here in the U.S.

3) **Women going topless being no big deal.** This was something I considered a "benefit" only during the time I was breast-feeding my two children (my husband considered this a benefit all of the time). After having experienced several months as a breast-feeding mother in the United States, I was amazed at the nonchalance with which it was treated in France. In the States I had to wear specially designed clothing and carry a drape with me at all times lest someone see my nipple (if only for

a millisecond) while I was feeding my baby. In Paris, on the bus, on the metro, even on the street, I regularly observed women who un- buttoned their blouses, whipped out a breast, and started to feed their child using no drape at all. Even more surprising was the fact that no one even seemed to notice the half-nude woman, and certainly no one gave her a hard time about exposing herself in public. I spent only three months as a breast-feeding mom in the United States, and I felt uncomfortable every single moment I did it. I could feel the eyes of the world upon me: men leering at me, old women giving me disapproving looks or a finger wag, as if to say, "Shame on you for doing that in public." It was discouraging and humiliating. Therefore, the freedom that came with breast-feeding my baby in a com- pletely accepting environment came as a wel- come surprise.

Within a few weeks of our arrival in Paris I had gone completely "native," whipping out my breast and feeding my baby whenever she needed to be fed and without even using a drape! It was an amazing, liberating feeling to be able to take care of my child's needs and not have to worry about when and where I was going to do it.

My husband had a bit of a harder time accept- ing the situation. I remember the first time he witnessed my European conversion. We were sitting on a bench waiting for a bus to take us back home after an all day excursion to La Défense. Carole started to cry, and I decided to see if she wanted to nurse. I lowered one shoulder of my peasant style blouse thus exposing my breast to public view. My husband immediately removed his baseball cap and held it just in front of my baby's head.

"What are you doing?" I said.

"I'm trying to cover up your nakedness" was his response.

"This is Europe," I said, swatting his hand away. "These people don't care about naked breasts!" I had come to realize what my French friend Fabienne had said was true: "You Americans are afraid of breasts."

I breast-fed my children for a combined total of eighteen months, and I was constantly amazed at how no one, not a single person, ever gave me a dirty look when I did so in public. Most just passed by without even noticing me or what I was doing. The only people who ever looked directly at me while I was breast-feeding my child were women, and when they saw what I was doing they would smile. It was like a huge weight was lifted from my shoulders. I never would have breast-fed my children for as long as I did had I not been living in Paris. I probably would have quit after just a couple of months, fed up with being stared at, harassed, and forced to retreat to a dirty, smelly restroom to feed my hungry baby.

4) **Going green.** We found it was easy to "go green" living in Paris since there were so many programs already in place that encourage green living. The government moved our car, along with all our furniture and possessions, to Europe, but we hardly ever used it. It sat in an underground parking garage for months at a time without use. I went to visit it every so often to make sure it was still there and to clean off some of the dust that had accumulated on the front and rear windshield. Our apartment was within walking distance of everything we needed on a daily basis: my older daughter's school, my younger daughter's day care center, the grocery store, the *boulangerie*, the pharmacy. If we needed to travel further than our own *arrondissement*, we took the metro.

The Paris metro system is legendary. It is efficient, extensive, and cheap. It runs from early in the morning to very late at night (late, at least, by American standards). When we moved back to the States, I was struck by how much time Americans spend in their cars, and I vowed to spend as little time as possible in mine. Thus, when it came time to buy a house, I insisted we buy a home in a neighborhood that was within walking distance to our children's schools, a grocery store, a pharmacy, and a bakery, just like our apartment in Paris!

We also got into the good habit of bringing our own bags to the grocery store since most places charge you a hefty per bag fee if you forget to bring something with you in which to lug home your purchases. After five years of always bringing our own reusable and recyclable bags to the grocery store, we never go anywhere without them.

5) **Public school starting at age three and affordable, quality day care.** This was probably the benefit we appreciated the most. Children can begin attending public school in France at age three for three hours a day, four mornings a week. The French also have a government subsidized day care program called a Halte Garderie. It is for children ages six weeks to three years and provides parents part-time day care for an hourly cost of approximately $1.85 per child. The children are grouped according to their age and spend their time making crafts, playing games, and singing adorable French songs. The *garderie* my older daughter attended even had an indoor play area complete with a slide and tricycles to ride around on. Both my daughters participated in this amazing program and enjoyed their time there immensely.

6) **Not so kid friendly.** There is actually an upside to this. Apparently the sound of babies

crying is the equivalent to fingernails scraping down a chalkboard to the French because they will do *anything* to make it stop. I discovered this quite by accident just a few months after we moved to Paris. In January of 2002, the euro replaced the franc as France's official currency. One of my tasks, as given to me by my husband, was to traipse across Paris with my six-month-old in tow to exchange our francs for euros. When I arrived at the central *Banque de France*, I entered into a giant, cavernous hall with a fifty-foot-tall ceiling. Rows and rows of bank teller windows stood opposite a single wooden bench upon which were perched two-dozen people. A machine spat out small paper tickets that indicated in what order we would each receive assistance. I pushed my stroller up to it and grabbed a ticket; I was number fifty-nine. A large black screen on the wall was illuminated by a red number thirty-two, the number currently being served. As I sat down at the end of the long bench resigned to a half hour wait or more, my normally very content daughter started to scream. Not cry. Scream.

I could not figure out what was wrong with her or what set her off, but no sooner had she started to wail than a short, balding man in a suit appeared at my side. He said simply, "Come with me, *madame*," and led me to the teller window closest to the exit. The teller was already busy with a customer, but *monsieur* stood there patiently until she was done. Then he said, "Please assist *madame*," and walked away. I was dumbfounded. I looked back at all the people we had just cut in front of, certain there was going to be some sort of outcry or protest, but there was none. The teller helped me with my transaction, and within three minutes of arriving at the bank I was out the door with my new euros in hand.

"And no one complained about you cutting in line, right?" said our French friend Bernard.

"Well, no," I replied.

"See, that could never happen in the States; people would complain."

Perhaps it's because Americans accept the fact that babies cry and kids whine as part of life, but here in the United States you don't get to skip to the front of the line just because your kids are making some unpleasant noise. Bernard was quick to point out as well that the bank personnel didn't necessarily want to help *me* as much as they wanted to help *themselves*. They were trying to get rid of the source of the noise so that their work environment was more pleasant, and everyone in the bank was complicit in achieving that goal. Even the people waiting in line, some of whom had arrived *well* before me, were happy to let me go ahead of them if it meant the screaming baby would go away sooner rather than later. It's kind of like passing the buck, except the buck is a person instead of some unpleasant task.

What I Don't Miss

1) **Public urination being commonplace.** One thing that I never got used to while living in Paris was the sight of individuals relieving themselves in public. While this type of behavior is to be expected of bums (either in Europe or Stateside) what was *unexpected* is the amount of well-dressed individuals I saw urinating on public streets. If I had a euro for every time I came across a well-dressed man standing with his johnson in his hand, urinating into the gutter (in full view of my two young children), I'd be a rich woman today. I always wanted to shout, "Sir, if you can afford that suit, you can afford to pay two euros to use a public toilet!" Apparently, this type of behavior is illegal but rarely punished because it's just not a big deal to the French.

2) **Nobody smiling.** Apart from the obvious reason (that you find something amusing), a smile in the United States can mean many things, among them "thank you," "hello, neighbor" or even "I sympathize with your situation." Not so in Paris. The French are very suspicious of random acts of kindness. Smiling can mean any or all of the following: 1) I know some illicit secret about you, 2) I'm after something that you have, or 3) I've recently undergone a full frontal lobotomy. If you are a woman,

there is also the added implication that you are interested in a casual sexual encounter. (I learned that one the hard way when I mistakenly smiled at a stranger who then proceeded to follow me around my *arrondissement* for twenty minutes while I completed my morning errands.)

I have to say I had a *really* hard time with this one simply because I'm a pretty happy person in general, and having spent the last thirty plus years of my life smiling almost every day made it difficult to quit cold turkey. I mean, how can you not walk around with a *constant* smile on your face when you live in one of the most beautiful cities on the planet?

3) **Not so kid friendly:** In Paris, children are seen as an annoyance, an accessory best left at home (with the nanny). There are very few "child friendly" restaurants in Paris, so taking our kids out to eat was an activity we rarely engaged in. Sadly, taking Carole to a matinee was also not an option, as the French rarely produce films for the ten-and-under set. If I wanted to take her to see a film that was age appropriate, I had to wait for an American movie to be released in France (which usually happened five to six months after its U.S. release date). Even more frustrating was the fact that they only showed the film in English at eight o'clock (or later) in the evening. Carole's bedtime for the first four years of her

life was seven o'clock, so she never saw an animated film in a movie theater until she was five.

Another seemingly "child friendly" activity is viewing the annual holiday themed decorated windows at the two famous Parisian department stores on the Right Bank: Printemps and Galeries Lafayette. Our apartment was just a few minutes' walk from them, and we delighted in taking Carole to see them the very first week in December every year. That is, until the year the display featured a *knife-wielding* madman. Each year the stores choose a particular theme for their window displays (Christmas apparently not being enough of a theme), and the December following Evelyn's birth the theme was fairytales. As we strolled by the windows, we watched Carole delight in viewing scenes from famous French fairytales such as "Puss in Boots," "Sleeping Beauty," and "Beauty and the Beast." However, her face became a mask of confusion when we reached the final window, which featured a beautiful blond princess seated at her make-up table. Standing directly behind her was a man dressed in regal robes and wearing a crown, holding a giant *dagger* in his hand. As we stood in silent horror, we watched the arm holding the dagger slowly move up and down as if he was stabbing the princess seated before him. We quickly ushered Carole away from the window before she could ask any disturbing questions about what she had just witnessed.

Once we arrived back at our apartment, I made a beeline for the computer and looked up the title of this fairytale that neither John nor I had ever heard of, "Peau d'Ane" (Donkeyskin). Turns out, it was written by Charles Perrault (the same author of "Cinderella" which makes one wonder what he was *smoking* at the time), and the story is quite similar but with a few very disturbing changes. A beautiful queen dies suddenly, but on her deathbed she makes her husband, the king, promise he will only remarry again if he can find a woman whose beauty equals her own. The king decides that only his daughter's beauty is equal to that of his late wife (her mother) and thus attempts to embark upon an incestuous relationship with her. As in "Cinderella," the girl's fairy godmother saves her from a dismal existence by advising the princess how to stall her father's advances long enough for her to escape the kingdom.

Now, the window displays at Galeries Lafayette and Printemps are decorated each year primarily for the enjoyment of *children*. In fact, special wooden steps and scaffolds are erected each year to elevate the youngest children several feet off the ground so they can get a better view. We had to ask ourselves, of all the French fairytales they could have depicted, whose idea was it to feature one involving incest? And even if they had no other choice but to use "Peau d'Ane" did they really have to choose a scene in which one character is trying to *murder* another? This incident is just one of many that happened to us in Paris where we as parents were left scratching our heads.

4) **Being unable to name your child anything you want.** There are lots of freedoms we Americans take for granted (something we became painfully aware of within just a few months of moving to Paris). However, this law was by far the most bizarre thing I had ever encountered in my life.

Giving birth in France forces one to come face-to-face with the antiquated rules regarding the name you can legally give your child. It had to be a name that already exists in French, so no creating your own moniker. Even the spelling of the child's name is scrutinized, as we soon found out. We chose to name our second daughter Evelyn. Turned out, Evelyn is actually a man's name (it came across the English Channel to France via the British writer Evelyn Waugh). In order to feminize the name (as they do with most nouns) the French simply added an E on the end. We, however, did not want our child to have this added E on the end of her name, as the

British spelling was far more common in the United States. This choice meant I was the recipient of harassment by nearly every single French person who came into contact with my newborn daughter at the hospital where she was born. "You're not allowed to spell it that way," they admonished me. Or, "That's a boy's name."

"Why aren't people allowed to give their child whatever name they choose?" I asked one particularly nasty nurse on duty.

"Because parents can't be trusted with such an important task," she snapped. And the criticism didn't end once we left the hospital. When I went to register her for day care, the director of the center also gave me a hard time about the misspelled name. "They only allowed you to do that because you are diplomats," she said matter-of-factly.

5) **The weather.** It rains a lot in Paris. And while Paris has lots of beautiful parks, they are less beautiful (and a lot less fun) while being pounded by a steady rain. Now, certainly there are a lot of cities in the world where it rains as much as Paris, but my biggest issue with the almost daily rain was the lack of indoor activities available for babies and young children. While living in Paris we did some traveling in and around the UK (a country notorious for rainy weather), and I was shocked and delighted at the vast array

of indoor activities available to parents with young children: indoor petting zoos, indoor go-kart tracks, cinemas that held kid- and baby-friendly movie screenings, and last but certainly not least pubs with a play area (no need to miss out on enjoying a pint of your favorite ale just because you can't get a babysitter!). Being cooped up in our apartment for days on end during the winter months gave all of us a bit of cabin fever.

6) **Turkish Toilets:** Also known as a Squat Toilet this type of toilet does not have an elevated seat and is essentially a *hole* in the ground. And while the city of Paris consistently uses elevated toilet seats in its public restrooms, the rest of France does not. Traveling in the French countryside during the weekend necessitated the use of roadside rest stops, which were often equipped with *only* Turkish Toilets. As a mother I can think of no more disturbing conversation than having to explain to one's three year old daughter how to use a Turkish Toilet. I mean, we are talking about the world's fifth largest economic superpower here, and a hole in the ground is the *best* they can do?

Chapter 15
My Paris Faves

Here is my list of the sights, shops, and eats in Paris that are not to be missed!

Manger

High tea at the Bristol: The ultimate in elegance and luxury. I sampled high tea at a dozen locations in Paris, and theirs is by far the best: filling and delicious. Oh, and did I mention they have *hot* waiters to boot? www.hotel-bristol.com

Mariage Frères: A Mecca for tea enthusiasts, Mariage Frères are the purveyors of the finest teas in the world. They have an astounding *four hundred* different kinds of tea on offer. There are several locations in Paris, but I recommend the Étoile location. It has a lovely boutique upstairs and a cozy tearoom downstairs, perfect for a Parisian lunch, *à deux*. www.mariagefreres.com

Le Soufflé: This cozy little restaurant located just off the Rue de Rivoli was one of our favorite places to take the many guests who came to visit us. As its name suggests, the main attraction here is soufflés, but they also have a wide selection of other exquisite French fare. The prices are very reasonable, and since this establishment is a favorite with American Embassy crowd, everyone speaks English! Reservations are not hard to get, but they are a must. www.lesouffle.fr

Convivium: Friends of ours who lived in the Seventeenth introduced us to this Sicilian Italian restaurant. The food is excellent, and the portions come in the larger sizes that most Americans are used to. But the main reason to visit this establishment is the atmosphere. Everyone is so friendly! From the coat-check girl to the waiters to the busboy, they could not be nicer. If you speak Italian you'll get a chance to use it during your meal here. They are open seven days a week and reservations are recommended. www.convivium.fr

Bateau Parisiens: This cruise features the most romantic dinner in the City of Lights. There are three classes of service: get the Premier. This ensures you'll have a small, intimate table for two reserved at the front of the boat (where the best views are to be had). You'll also get a dedicated waiter whose only job is to make sure your wine glass is always full. Is it pricey? Yup! But how often are you in Paris? Tell the husband to suck it up and book it. Oh, and when the waiter asks what kind of *apéritif* you'd like, ask for an *Élysées*. www.bateauxparisiens.com

Eric Kayser: The week after we arrived in Paris, the *boulangerie* across the street from our apartment abruptly closed. It was replaced a month later by an Eric Kayser. At the time we had no idea how lucky we were. Their baguettes and croissants are truly the best in Paris. And if you are looking for a gourmet lunch at a bargain price, this is the place. My friend Megan, the professional chef, says it's the best twenty-five-euro lunch she's *ever* had. They serve only breakfast and lunch and do not take reservations. www.erickayser.com

La Durée: Welcome to pastry heaven. Famous in Paris for their *macarons* (delicate meringue cookies which bear no resemblance to the dense coconut macaroons Americans are familiar with) this company has been tempting the taste buds of Parisians since 1862. There are several locations in Paris. I prefer the one on the Champs-Élysées since it is the only one with a *twenty-five-foot-long* pastry counter. And don't be afraid to ask the smartly dressed employees behind the counter to explain, in detail, each and every pastry before making your decision. www.laduree.com

PS: Make sure you get a box of *macarons* to take home with you. Caramel and coconut are my personal favorites.

Maille: Mustard is very important to the Parisians. And who knew there were so many different kinds? Not only do they wrap and package every purchase beautifully, they give you a brochure (in English or *en Français*) that tells you exactly which mustards go with which types of food. You *must* visit this store if for no other reason than to see mustard dispensed from a *spigot* mounted on the counter! www.maille.com

A Faire:

Agatha Paris: Unique, stylish, good quality jewelry that won't break the bank—and that's saying something in this city! Whenever I needed a new set of earrings or a hip necklace, Agatha was the place I went. www.agatha.fr

Parc Monceau: Picturesque Paris moments abound in this quiet oasis in the Eighth. We were lucky enough to live just down the street and visited it nearly every day. There are pony rides every afternoon, a huge waterfall, a romantic stone bridge over a tranquil pond, and a newly refurbished play area for the kids. Buy some baguette sandwiches at the Kayser *boulangerie* located just down the street, then grab a bench and watch your kids play contentedly for hours! It is the best *free* entertainment in Paris.

Hermès: And speaking of free...my friend Ileana introduced me to this fabulous idea. Head over to the Hermès boutique at 24 Rue Faubourg St. Honoré (the one that famously refused Oprah Winfrey entry) and head straight to the perfume counter. Tell the exceedingly polite personnel behind the counter that you're interested in their fine perfumes, but you'd like to try some on before buying. They will spray a signature brown satin Hermès ribbon with the scent of your choice and then carefully wrap your wrist and forearm in the scented satin. The lovely fragrance will stay with you all day, and you get a nice souvenir to take home. And believe me, that lovely satin logo ribbon is the only thing you'll *ever* get for free at an Hermès store. www.hermes.com

Bois de Rose: Located in the Latin Quarter, Bois de Rose specializes in gorgeous, hand-embroidered smocked clothing for boys and girls. Their clothes are made from the highest quality fabrics in a dizzying array of colors. Whether you are shopping for a newborn, toddler, or child up to age twelve, you'll fall in love with the clothes at this boutique (I know I did). They will even create matching dresses for your daughter and her favorite doll! 30 Rue Dauphine, Paris, Sixth.

Bouchara: From silk Jaquard to Toile de Jouy, this store sells the finest fabrics assembled all under one roof. I purchased several meters of bright *Provençal* prints and had them made into table linens for our breakfast nook. www.bouchara.com

Creed: Makers of fine perfume for over two hundred and fifty years, they specialize in sophisticated scents that are anything but commonplace. If you are looking for a unique perfume that not everyone else is wearing, then a visit to this boutique is a must. 38 Avenue Pierre 1er de Serbie, Eighth.

8216090R0

Made in the USA
Lexington, KY
15 January 2011